Between the Knives

A Missionary's Story

By

Dot Alvord

Table of Contents

Dedication

This book is dedicated to Alec, who gave me strength,
encouragement, but mostly love for 63 years and for all of eternity.

About the Cover

The drawing on the cover of my book is an original artwork from Alec. He loved Africa and its people. And he was very creative with his drawings.

The drawing is of African people working to "beat their swords in to plowshares and their spears in to pruning hooks." Rhodesia, and much of Africa, was experiencing conflict while we lived and worked there. They were trying to achieve peace as an independent country. As missionaries, we came to Rhodesia to show the people the way to ultimate peace, through Jesus Christ.

The tree in the artwork is the msasa tree, indigenous to Zimbabwe. The msasa tree is a broad tree and often grows in the savanna of Zimbabwe. The name in the Venda language of Zimbabwe means "the one left behind." The people of Rhodesia were left behind from self-rule until they gained their independence in 1980.

Finally, the initials in the bottom right are from Alec. He always used a double A on his artwork and sketches. Using his artwork on the cover of my book is a loving tribute to a faithful servant of God.

Introduction

Knives have been used for centuries. The knife was one of the first tools used by humans. They are used in cooking, in eating the cooked food, in hunting and fishing, in crafts, and so many other areas. Imagine trying to live without a knife.

Knives are, unfortunately not just helpful but have been used for evil at times. Knives have been used for self-harm and harm to others. Recently in the news there was a story telling of a young woman who was murdered. Her assailant used a machete. Bloody wars have included knives, spears, swords, and bayonets.

Knives come in different materials. The earliest knives were made from bone. Now, most knives have transitioned to blades made from different materials. They all need to be sharpened to be effective. Some knives have plain, utilitarian handles, while others are ornate. Knives may come in sets or be uniquely, individually designed, and crafted.

They are part of our lives, whether we look for them or not. Regardless of the material or whether they are used for good or evil, knives all belong to the same class of tools.

This is the story of Dorothy Weems Alvord, a United Methodist Missionary serving in what was Southern Rhodesia. At the time that she was in missions, Southern Rhodesia was part of the Central Africa Federation which also included Northern Rhodesia and Nyasaland. Northern Rhodesia is now Zambia and Nyasaland is Malawi. Southern Rhodesia is today an independent Zimbabwe.

These pages tell of mission life and work during the war-torn years of Zimbabwe's emerging independence. The common thread throughout the book is TRANSITION. As the country moved closer to independence, missionaries were replaced by national leaders.

This is her story of living through transition, between the knives. Both good and bad.

PART I: Called By Name

"Now thus says the Lord, He who created you, O Jacob, He who formed you, O Israel:

Fear not, for I have redeemed you

I have called you by name, you are mine."

Isaiah 43:1 (RSV)

Chapter One: Childhood

We will not hide the teachings of God from their children but tell to the coming generations the glorious deeds of the Lord, and his might and the wonders that he has wrought done. Psalms 78:4 (RSV).

The task of this book is to tell my faith story to future generations. The title of the first section of my story comes from Nancy Higgs, a devout Methodist woman from the North Alabama Conference in the United States. She was writing a book that sprung from the hymn, "I Love to Tell the Story". She invited each missionary from the North Alabama Conference who had served under the General Board of Global Missions to submit their story. She asked each person to speak to their calling from God to be a missionary. I sent Nancy my entry for her book, and she named my story, CALLED BY NAME.

God's claim on my life began very early. The naming of the first-born child of Jimmie Lou Steadmon and Connie Norton Weems created awareness that I had been given the name Dorothy because it meant Gift of God. The year was 1937 in Town Creek, Alabama, a part of Lawrence County. When I was born my parents were living next door to the Donald Baptist Church. It was this church that we related to as long as my parents lived on the farm of my grandfather and worked there with other members of my father's family. My paternal grandparents, Mr. and Mrs. Ed Weems were Baptist people. I am not certain what denomination my maternal grandparents, Mr., and Mrs. John Steadmon, were. Any church seemed to fit them. Some of my earliest memories included watching my dad sharpen his straight edge razor on Saturday evenings as he was preparing to shave and get ready to teach Sunday School the next day.

While the name given to me by my parents was Dorothy, I was known in the family and the community as Dottie. When I reached the age of reason my mother told me she had a vision that I would "walk the world reading the Bible." She read to me Colossians 3:17, "And whatever you do, in word and deed, do everything in the name of the Lord Jesus, giving thanks to God the Father through him." My parents always kept before me that I was a gift from God. I began to feel God calling me by name through the voices of my family. My father came from a family of eleven and six of the siblings were teachers. I had two great-aunts that taught in the local county high school. They were my role models. At age four, I ordered my first "pupil" from the Sears Roebuck catalogue because I wanted to be a teacher like my great-aunts. I thought everything came from the Sears Roebuck catalog. But this pupil was different though. He was human. He was my brother, Lindsey. It was later that I found out that he did not come from the catalog. As we grew, we were great friends.

Dot and her first "pupil," her brother Lindsey.

The Second World War came and Norton, my father, along with his nine brothers went to war, leaving me, my baby brother Lindsey Lee and mother in a house on Sixth Avenue in Decatur, Alabama. Our house was so close to Ninth Street Methodist Church I could hear the people singing if my bedroom window was open. My friends, Linda Gayle Smith, Alice Gene Owens, and Nancy Reeder went to that church. I spent my young life at the Methodist Church, the Church of God at the corner and at the Baptist Church on the next block. I would play with other children that gathered on these sacred pieces of ground.

When my maternal grandparents came to live with us my Grandpa John made a path to the Ninth Street Methodist Church. "Brother John" as he was called, was always called on to pray. I can remember that he ended each prayer with these words, "IN OUR REDEEMER'S NAME." He always ran the words together and I never really knew what it meant until I was an adult. Every mention of my name by my grandparents was followed by a reminder that I was a gift from God.

Much to my joy, my parents permitted me to have piano lessons from the Methodist minister's wife, Mrs. Oppie Gamble. This put me in the presence of a member of that church once a week. She taught me using the red Thompson song book. I learned hymns and then other types of music.

While at piano lessons, I heard the news that my friends were all going to summer camp. I wanted to go with them, but I needed to be a member of their church in order to go and have my way paid by the church. I joined that church without asking my parents. They were not happy when I told them about joining the church. But what could they do? I went to camp with my Methodist friends on a scholarship from the church.

Chapter Two: Youth

Don't let anyone look down on you because you are young, but set an example for the believers in speech, in conduct, in love, in faith and in purity. 1 Timothy 4:12 (GNTD)

My parents bought a restaurant in Hartselle, Alabama and we spent the early 1950's in Hartselle, just 12 miles from Decatur. I attended the First Methodist Church in Hartselle and continued my summer camp experiences with friends through the eighth and ninth grades. My dearest friend during those years was Ila Jo Wallace, a second daughter of a devout Baptist family. As teenagers we read the Bible and prayed together. Occasionally I would have an invitation to sleep over at her house. She could not come to my house as my parents were involved with the restaurant most of the time. I would get an invitation to go to the Gospel Singings in Birmingham with her family. Her father was a minister of music. These experiences continued to add to the "building blocks" of my calling.

My piano lessons with Mrs. Gamble really paid off, literally. In the restaurant there was a piano and I played songs while the diners ate. I played all kinds of music, from country to gospel, and the diners gave me tips. My musical diversity continued to grow as the patrons of the restaurant had requests for certain songs. Also, during this time, I played the clarinet in the school band. And I was busy in the theatrical parts. The school I was attending produced a play titled, "Grandad Steps Out" by Felicia Metcalfe. I had a major part as Tilley, a nosy maid from across the street who tattled on the grandfather who was sneaking out of the house for a dinner with friends. It was a lot of fun. What wasn't fun was that my nickname in school was "Wormy". All my friends called me that because my last name was Weems and they thought it was funny. I played basketball in school, and they would start yelling "Wormy!" whenever I got the ball. Another thing I loved was roller skating. There was a roller-skating rink right next door to the restaurant. Because of my musical talent, I was able to skate very easily to the music at the local rink. In fact, I became a champion figure roller skater and won some trophies. Altogether, music was part of my life and would be part of my ministry.

Dot, Middle School

Dot, Roller Skating Champion

10

Dot, Marching Band outfit   Dot, High School Graduation

In 1952 my parents moved again, this time to Birmingham, Alabama, 70 miles from Hartselle. This move caused a sharp pain because I was leaving my good friend Ila Jo. We rented a parsonage home that was not being used by the pastor in the city called Central Park. I became a part of the Central Park Methodist Church. It was in the parsonage with Pastor Woodfin and Dorothy Grove that I first shared my feelings of God's claim on my life. I felt the call to full time Christian Service and publicly shared the assurance of the call. As a teen, I was given a youth membership in the Women's Society of Christian Service (WSCS). I taught Sunday school, was a part of the Methodist Youth Fellowship (MYF) and Youth Representative on the Board of Stewards. I was given scholarships to attend summer camp and many other opportunities to learn about the church. It was during this time that I realized that I wanted to be a teacher, but I wanted to be a missionary teacher and I felt called to Africa.

It was in 1953 my dear friend from Hartselle, Ila Jo, came with her dad to the Birmingham Barons baseball game. I met them and attended the game with them. Jo was permitted to spend the night and catch the Greyhound bus home the next day. This was a very unusual visit because we had never had the opportunity for her to visit me or stay overnight. The happiness of being with my dearest friend was indescribable.

In the very early hours of Sunday, her father called. Jo's mother was very ill and her dad and older sister, Reita, were taking her to Nashville Baptist Hospital. Ila Jo would need to go home as soon as possible. Her Uncle Alton would be waiting for her when she got off the bus and then they would drive to Nashville. Jo was amazed at the fact that I, her sixteen-year-old best friend, knew how to catch a city bus (she lived on a farm) and get her on a Greyhound bus to return home safely. Another intense separation from a beloved friend.

But this is another reminder of how God takes care of His children. God allowed Ila Jo and me to keep in touch over the years as we have served Him around the world and the friendship never ends. Our friendship has lasted over sixty years.

Central Park Methodist supported Miss Annie Parker, a missionary in Africa. Each year we would have an Annie Parker Day, to celebrate our partnership. I would see and hear her and feel that God was calling me to do that same work.

It was during this time Miss Lois Mildred Taylor came home to Alabama from Rhodesia. She was serving as a Methodist missionary under the General Board of Global ministries of the Methodist Church. She was a contemporary of my parents since they went to school together. My family went to hear her speak when she was home on furlough. During one visit she gave me the names of some of her students to be my pen pals. After writing for years, we began to talk of the possibility of visiting one another. In her correspondence she sent the story called The Legend of the Black Madonna. It is included in the appendix of this book because it speaks so much to her desire that we all be one in the family of God. She called everyone FRIEND.

It is interesting that her primary focus during her retirement was her active membership in the Church of the Reconciler, a new multicultural/interracial United Methodist Church in downtown Birmingham served by her pastor Rev. Dr. Lawton Higgs Sr. He always made it possible for her to live out her call through the outreach of the church in retirement. My precious mentor, "Big Sister" Dr. Lois Mildred Taylor died in Birmingham, Alabama. She was 87 years old and served 39 of those years as a General Board of Global Ministries missionary in Zimbabwe and Botswana.

Not only was it missionaries coming home and sharing their stories that I discerned my call, but it was also our own conference youth ministries led by Nina Reeves through whom God continued to call me. She used musical games with us for recreational time. She was a role model for me, but she did not know it. I dreamed of having a copy of those records and leading young people as she did. Years later my church at Central Park in Birmingham bought those records for me and I used them as a caravanner.

Chapter Three: Young Adult

I press on toward the goal to win the prize for which God has called me heavenward in Christ Jesus. Philippians 3:14 (NIV)

What was a Youth Caravan? This was a program that spanned 21 years (1939-1959) and had involved more than five thousand people—youth and adults, hundreds of churches, and thousands of local church youth. This program was one of the most meaningful experiences of my young adult life. To be a part of a Caravan Team, three girls, one boy, one adult, visiting local churches, making more effective the work of the church with youth was producing a call for me.

Its purpose was to reach every important religious problem of youth, both personal and social. Harvey Brown, writing in a church publication in 1950 after telling how many people had been involved in Caravanning in eleven years, said, "This is a record of volunteer service which is unequaled by any church or religious organization in Christendom." During its existence, it was hailed by those working with youth as one of the most successful programs that the Methodist Church had ever had.

The basic purpose of the Youth Caravan idea was the heart of Christianity—to serve. And the Caravanners did—for a summer, without pay. We received financial support for expenses only. I owe a debt to Paul B. Kern, Paul Worley, Walter Towner, Harvey Brown, Lillian Hay, Hoover Rupert, Joe Bell, Harold Ewing and many, many others. God used this work of the church to call me into missionary service. My caravan sister, Kathy Kelly Bryant told this gripping story to our youth on Friday night at the closing service.

The Yellow Mackinaw (Windbreaker)

It was one of those cold, wet, dreary evenings when a young man had a serious accident. It was so serious that it was necessary to call a specialist doctor from a city quite a distance from there.

The doctor began his long journey and passing through one town he saw a man hitch-hiking. This part of the country was strange to him so he thought he would like to have some company. So, he stopped and asked the man to get in. He saw that the man had on an old dirty yellow mackinaw, dirty gloves and had a three-day growth of beard. The man piled in the back seat and did not say anything. Several times the doctor tried to strike up a conversation with him, but the man would not say much. The doctor began to get a little nervous and he was soon to find out his feelings were justified. The man stuck a gun in the doctor's ribs and said, "O.K. buddy, pull over to the side of the road." The doctor thought it would be better to be late at the hospital than never to get there at all, so he did as he was told. He got out of the car and watched it pull away into the dark rainy night.

It was some time before the doctor was able to get help and reach the hospital. As he entered the door, he saw two local doctors coming out of the surgery and he knew by looking at them that it was too late. He approached the doctors, and they began to tell him about the case. Presently one of the other doctors said, "Oh, we want you to meet the boy's father."

They went into the waiting room and there sat a man wearing an old dirty yellow mackinaw, dirty gloves and had a three-day growth of beard on his face.

Do we push the one out of our lives that we are called to serve?

This story has never left me. I have forever asked myself, "Do I push God out of my life?" Oh! God let me always be about serving you. "Go ye," was becoming so real!

Another very meaningful God experience came during Caravanning. On the night of July 10, 1957, a stranger walked into Trinity Methodist Church in Wise, Virginia where the Caravan was working. Finding the door open he walked in and spent a while meditating at the altar although the church was dark and there was no one to show him the way. After his prayer he wrote a short note to express gratitude for the opportunity to pray at the altar, he had found God and was leaving fifty cents on the altar. The church leaders later decided to prepare, with the stranger's gift, a small light with an extension cord and a bulb to put a perpetual light at the altar.

I was accepted to attend Birmingham Southern College. My plan was to get a Bachelor of Art in Philosophy with a minor in Religion. I planned to complete my studies in three years instead of four to save money. To prepare financially for college, I worked with the girls' volleyball team at the local Catholic Church. I coached the younger girls' team and was a referee for the older girls' games. I was paid for this work and saved everything I could for college. On Mondays I had a paid position at the Methodist church. I received $75 each month. I was bonded by the church which allowed me to take the empty offering envelopes and record the amounts given to the church. The treasurer took the money on Sundays and deposited it in the bank.

Again, all money that I earned was earmarked for college. I was also blessed to receive a scholarship from the WSCS (Women's Society of Christian Service) from my church. God affirmed and confirmed that I was on the right path because I had enough money for college.

While at Birmingham Southern, I began to prepare for missions. I studied French because I felt the call to go to the Congo. And the language there was French. After the summer of working with the Caravan, I applied to the Women's Division of the Board of Missions in New York. They were recruiting young adults in colleges across the states. I was a part of the Methodist Student Movement at Birmingham Southern and I had just been to Lawrence, Kansas, to a gathering of our organization. The call was to students who wanted to serve three years as short-term missionaries to apply for service. This program was called The 3's since the commitment was for three years. My application was accepted, and I was assigned to meet the Personnel Committee in Atlanta, GA, for an interview. I was accepted and told to attend the training to be held at Scarritt College in the summer of 1958.

Chapter Four: Marriage

For this reason, a man will leave his father and mother and be united to his wife, and the two will become one flesh. Ephesians 5:31 (NIV)

Summer Romance.

The training for mission service began at DePauw University in Greencastle, Indiana, June 19, and then we would move on to Scarritt College in Nashville, Tennessee. While at DePauw, I was assigned with several other young women to prepare for mission service in Southern Rhodesia, not the Congo. I had prepared to go to the Congo, but God was making a straight path to a different area. My desire to go to the mission field was the primary motive. Where I would go was secondary. I would have willingly gone anywhere that my advisors felt was the place for me.

A young man would be joining our group. Alec arrived late as he had to stay at the Pacific School of Religion for graduation. He showed up wearing a dashiki and the group of us assigned to Rhodesia could not help but laugh. And he talked funny, which made us laugh harder. Little did we know that Alec would become a very important part of our preparation in the 3's program. Later, when we learned that he was born in Rhodesia, we all realized that God was leading us, and Alec.

Alec's parents, Emory Delmont, and Berniece had been serving in Africa since 1919. They never returned to the states to live, only to visit. Alec's father was born in Park City, Utah, and was an agriculturist. His mother, from Norfolk, Nebraska, was a kindergarten teacher. Their story is recorded in a book by Clarence W. Hall entitled Adventurers for God, published by Harper & Brothers, Publishers, New York, in 1959. The story is entitled "The Gospel of the Plow." They had five children born in Southern Rhodesia and in Mozambique. Alec was the only child that chose to leave Africa for his education. All the other children remained in Africa for their education. After sixty years of work in Southern Rhodesia, they died there and were buried in the land they served and loved.

After our time at DePauw, on July 2nd, as we were preparing to load the buses to go to Scarritt, Alec asked me to sit with him. We talked all the way. He shared all about Rhodesia and his family. His parents were missionaries in what was Southern Rhodesia at the time, where I would be going for my missionary service. His parents had sent Alec, the youngest child of the family, as a seventeen-year-old to live with his mom's brother, Don. His four siblings and their families were at that time living in Southern Rhodesia. The bus ride was 478 miles and nine hours. Just as we were pulling into Nashville Alec proposed to me. I made him wait a few days as I thought about it. On July 4th I accepted Alec's proposal. Alec always called me Dot. Never Dorothy or Dottie, and definitely not Wormy, but Dot. He called me by name to be his bride, just as God had called me by name to be in mission for Him.

Alec and I told the Women's Division of our plans to marry, and we were told that we could not continue with The 3's program. That program was designed for young, single people. Now that we were going to be married, if we still felt a call to mission service, we would have to change to the Career Missions program and that meant a five-year commitment. Neither of us had any doubt. While our program

19

changed, our field of mission service did not. We would still be going to Rhodesia.

We planned an August 14 Engagement Party in Norfolk, Nebraska at the home of Aunt Bess and Uncle Don as they had been surrogate parents for Alec. Alec and Uncle Don had many quality hours together. They played card games and board games often.

Since it was short notice and a long distance, all his family in Southern Rhodesia were unable to be a part of our wedding plans. I took the train by myself from Alabama to Nebraska. Alec was already there to meet me. Our engagement appeared in local papers in Birmingham and Hartselle, Alabama.

After meeting the family and celebrating our engagement, on August 20, Alec left for Pennsylvania, to begin his appointment serving two churches in the Central New York Conference, the Big Pond/Wetona Charge, under the District Superintendent, Dr. Phil Torrance. I went to Alabama to complete my last quarter of college for my degree, I would graduate in December 1958 with a Bachelor of Arts in Religion and Philosophy. During this time, my mother cut a pattern for my wedding dress. She used the "funny papers" which are the comics included in a lot of newspapers. It was a special time when she was working on my wedding dress.

On November 16, the WSCS of the Central Park Methodist Church gave us a Miscellaneous Tea Shower. It was a start to what has become for us the making of a beautiful store of wedding gifts and memories. Many times, in our international travels, we have needed to leave these items stored in Alabama while we served overseas. But the pain of leaving them behind turned to joy because they have always been available when we were back in the United States on furlough.

On December 7, our wedding was held at Central Park Methodist Church at 10:50 am, just after the morning Worship service, which ended at 10:45 am. We had communion during Worship. At the end of worship, Brother Grant Parris asked us to come forward. Unfortunately, Brother Woodfin Grove was moved from Central Park. We had planned the wedding with him but needed to have his successor, Brother Grant Parris, to conduct the ceremony. It was hard to be married by a minister that did not know us very well.

Uncle Don and Aunt Bess from Nebraska came for the wedding. Grandmother Weems, who I lovingly called "Mommy" came with my mother and father to the wedding. Norma Gene Turner was my maid of honor and Hunter Mabry was Alec's best man. We had a small private reception at my home. We only had time to serve wedding cake. We were to board the 2pm train to Pennsylvania where Alec was serving. While my mother was making my wedding dress, she also made my Going Away outfit. It was a beautiful blue wool with a fur collar.

Dot and Alec's Wedding Day, with Norma Gene Turner, Maid of Honor, and Hunter Mabry, Best Man.

Family Gathering at the Wedding. (l to r front row) Alec, Dot, Grandmother Weems, Norton Weems. (l to r back row) Uncle Don, Aunt Bess, Jimmie Lou Weems

My Going Away outfit made by my mom.

We boarded the train, knowing the trip would take 12 hours. No honeymoon for us. But we talked the entire time, and the time flew. Someone from Alec's church met us in Big Pond, Pennsylvania at 2 am. They drove us to the parsonage. It was a very cold night, and the bedroom upstairs had no heat. But we snuggled. It was a wonderful beginning to our married life together.

Then we got the painful news that Uncle Don had a heart attack after the wedding. He died, leaving Aunt Bess to make her agonizing trip back to Nebraska on her own. It was a sad time. We went from having the high of just being married and then the extreme low of losing a surrogate parent. We were not able to go to Nebraska for the funeral.

During this time after our marriage, I had been given a substitute teaching position at Springfield Elementary school. The administrators at the school had worked with Birmingham Southern College to provide a proctor in Pennsylvania so that I could complete my final exams. I received my degree in abstention. I was not able to attend the graduation, not able to celebrate all the hard work I had done to achieve my degree. But I had finished. I had planned to complete my degree in three years, and I did it. I saved money and had a huge life transition.

We had been told by the Board of Missions we would need to serve a year together in the States before we were sent overseas. We were willing to follow their directives. Our commissioning service was set for January 1959 in Buck Hill Falls, Pennsylvania. During that time, we found out the truth of Walter Scott's words, "Love is the most enriching ingredient of life."

One of the traditions of the people in our new community was to always give newlyweds a horning bee. The horning bee was an event where the newlyweds would be surprised by visitors and the young couple were supposed to have food and beverage for the guests. The ones doing the horning bee would come into the house and play tricks on the newlyweds (tie up the sheets etc.). It did not sound like a lot of fun to us but one of the local people told me when it was scheduled to happen. Someone let the cat out of the bag as the old saying goes, and I was able to have food ready when the pranksters got there. Luckily, some of those that would be coming also brought food. Thank goodness the horning bee only happened once, and we survived the fun.

I began to substitute teach in the thirteen schools in Bradford County, Pennsylvania. I only missed teaching on the days we were snowed in. We heard the story about the year before we came when the area had a huge snowstorm. The children were out of school for three weeks. Stores ran low on food and supplies so that items had to be dropped from helicopters to some residents. We hoped that snowstorm would not repeat itself while we were in Pennsylvania. Because I was substituting at different schools each day, Alec would drive me to the school I was assigned to cover for the day and then at the end of the day he would pick me up. In between he would visit parishioners or work at the church. It was a special time to have him take care of me like this.

When teaching first grade with forty-one students, I contracted measles. I was afraid and my doctor told me I needed to have an injection of gamma globulin since I was pregnant. Right after that time I had to start wearing glasses because the measles affected my eyes. Alec was driving me to the doctor's office to get the injection when a heifer crossed the road in front of the car. The car was demolished. The cow died. In this area there was a closed pasture law which meant the owner of the animal had to pay for the damage. We were able to get a rental car to finish out our time serving the charge. Thankfully, I got the injection and got over the measles. But we still had to wait about five months to see if the baby would have any issues from my measles.

On Wednesday nights we held Bible Study at the parsonage. I was in the kitchen preparing some refreshment when one of the ladies told me I needed some maternity clothes as my dress was too tight. The following day Alec took me shopping. I fainted in Ben Franklin dime store in Troy, Pennsylvania while buying maternity clothes. As a teenager I had fainting spells and now that I was pregnant, I had them again. I had been on my feet a lot that day and was a little dehydrated. The ambulance was called, and I was taken to the hospital. I stayed in the hospital for several days, recuperating and getting some fluids to hydrate me. The following Wednesday night I put on the maternity clothes that I had purchased. Another of the women followed me into the kitchen she said, "Honey, you shouldn't put on maternity clothes too early, you may not have that baby." It was at this very early stage in my life as a pastor's wife that I learned I could not please all the parishioners. I just cried and Alec was so loving and reassured me to do what I felt best. Another one of those times when knives were crossed, and I was between them. I learned that people would be telling me different things about situations, and I would need to trust my common sense and God to make the right decision.

Dot, pregnant with their first child, in Pennsylvania

There was a very devout mother, named Faith Leonard, in our Big Pond Church. She had one child, a boy of sixteen. She could only look down on the parking lot from her third-floor sanitarium room and order clothes for him out of the Sears Catalog. She was isolated because she had tuberculosis. When he got his driving license, he had an accident and was killed. That mother taught me so much about unconditional love and faith that I asked her permission to name our first child Faith.

We received a wire from Africa telling us Alec's father, Emory Durland, had died in Southern Rhodesia. We had only been married for a few months and I had never met his dad. In our short time together, Alec has lost his father and his surrogate parent. The pain was a dagger to our hearts. We wired the Board of Missions telling of his father's death. A returned wire gave us permission to leave for Africa in twenty-four hours. Our church members at Big Pond helped us pack. The people of our community were helpful in getting barrels from a local pickle company and building frames to pack our belongings in. We were supposed to be in Pennsylvania for one year. But this caused us to go to the mission field early. In just a matter of hours we were in an airplane heading to Southern Rhodesia. We did not get there in time for the funeral which left us sad, but the trip was ending with us being with family. That was a blessing. It was also a nervous time because I would be meeting Alec's family for the first time.

Chapter Five: Flight to Rhodesia

It was the Lord our God himself who brought us and our parents up out of Egypt, from that land of slavery, and performed those great signs before our eyes. He protected us on our entire journey and among all the nations through which we traveled. Joshua 24:17 (NIV)

We were off to Southern Rhodesia for our first term of service which was to be five years. The trip was a flight of about 10,000 miles over a three-day period. I was five months pregnant. I had flown before, when going from Birmingham to Atlanta when I was being first evaluated for mission work. This flight was very different. Today, airplanes can fly from the United States to Africa without stopping. But in 1959, we had to stop several times to get fuel for the plane. When the plane stopped for fuel, we would disembark for the time it took for the refueling. Then we would get back on the plane and resume our trip. In Frankfort, Germany, at one of the stops, I had some milk to drink. Unfortunately, it was not very fresh, and it ended up upsetting my stomach. The rest of the flight was very uncomfortable. I had many periods of nausea and vomiting.

As the plane touched down in Khartoum, Sudan, we disembarked while the plane was refueled. It seemed as if the very hot steaming ground and the hot air we were breathing would consume us. It was my first experience on the soil of that great golden continent of Africa. Little did I know that Africa would be our home for the most of twenty years. We had no idea what was ahead, it was that walk of faith with the Lord after you answered, "Here I am Lord, send me."

Finally, we landed in Salisbury, in Rhodesia. This was where Alec's family was living, and I was about to meet his mother, siblings, and other family members. When we met, I was welcomed, and expressions of love were lavished on me as if I had been a part of the family forever. As a family, we grieved the loss of Alec's father.

We were only going to be with the family for a few days because we had been assigned to the Language School at Nyakatsapa. We would be there from May 31 through August 26 to learn the language of the people. Nyakatsapa is in the eastern district of Southern Rhodesia, in sight of Watsomba Mountain. It was standard procedure that all new missionaries learn to speak the language before receiving an appointment. Since Alec has grown up in Rhodesia, he was familiar with the different dialects. He knew Chinchou and Ndebele language, but he had to learn the language in Rusape where we were to serve. He still had to attend language school.

The official language of Southern Rhodesia was English, and the official African language was Shona. But the language of the area where we would serve was Chimanyika. Earl Stevick wrote the lessons for Chimanyika which included the informal language of the people. Machiwana served as chief tutor and wrote the lessons for the more formal structure and grammar of Shona. We had to be prepared to speak Shona when we left our region and traveled to Salisbury for meetings with the church officials.

There were six pods of missionaries at the language school. We had formal classes in the morning with Miss Ila Scovill, directress of the school. In the afternoon we were assigned an informant who gave us practical lessons in the language by engaging us in community life. Each afternoon we practiced what we learned in the class. My informant was a young adult my same age, promised in marriage. We

29

became fast friends. Her name was Shebbaoh Chidzekwe and her reputation and skills as a teacher were at stake with my learning. If I didn't pass the course, she may not be given another missionary to work with and she would lose her job.

She arranged for me to be fully immersed in the work of the village. At one time, I went to the river to help wash clothes. I did like the other women and took off my clothes and got in the river with them. During this time, I was able to converse with the local women in their language, and we talked about those universal things that women talk about all over the world: family, children, and husbands. Shebbach also arranged for me to help with replacing of a thatched roof on one of the homes in the area. I was pregnant so I could not climb up to the top of the hut. I carried the straw to the men who then placed it on the roof. Again, I was able to converse in the local language. Other things that Shebbaoh arranged was working in a garden and gathering vegetables and then cooking them with local women. All of this was done to immerse ourselves, not just in the language, but the culture of the area.

My exam was arranged with the local church for a day to preach, read the scripture and pray. I was so nervous and felt so responsible for Shebbach. I just could not fail. I passed the course and Shebbach was going to keep her job.

After language school, we were off to Rusape to begin our first term of service after completing our exams. The desire to learn and be engaged with God in His work was never greater in all my life. This was what I was meant to do. God had been present in what was a call for Alec, a call for me and now we were married. We were ready to begin work on the appointment given by the Bishop of the Rhodesian Annual Conference.

PART II: "Go Ye: Telling the Story"

Go therefore and make disciples of all nations, baptizing them in the name of the Father and of the Son, and of the Holy Spirit, and teaching them to obey everything that I have commanded you. And remember I am with you always, to the end of the age.

Matthew 28: 19-20 (NRSV)

Chapter Six: Church Work

Let us not give up the habit of meeting together, as some are doing. Instead, let us encourage one another all the more, since you see that the day of the Lord is coming nearer. Hebrews 10:25 (GNTD)

Rusape is a small town situated on the main Salisbury/Umtali/Beira Road about 105 miles from Salisbury, the capital city. It is fifty-seven miles from Umtali and 250 miles from Beira. It is the center of an important agricultural area, specializing in maize, tobacco, cattle, and fruit. Rusape has a well-diversified industrial area. The town is well served by shops and the residential area is well planned and comprised of some attractive houses. A large mining complex was being developed by the Headlands area nearby. The climate of the area varies considerably with the altitude. Rusape itself is 4,126 feet above sea level and has a pleasant, healthy and for most of the year, a cool climate. Parts of the area are as high as 6,000 feet above sea level, and in such places the climate is for the most part bracing and cool, not at all what people usually think about when they picture Africa.

When we arrived, there were few businesses: a grocery store, a drug store, a butcher, post office and a hospital, in addition to churches and schools. The road was paved, which distinguished it from smaller villages. There was a large open air African bus station four blocks out of town. They had every size, shape, and color of buses. Buses would come in and people would get off and others would get on. The buses took people all over Rhodesia. The bus would stop in the middle of a road and people would get off and just start walking down a dirt path, no village in sight. On top of the bus was a section where people put their items. There were loads of laundry, bicycles, or crates of livestock. One time I saw a goat on top of the bus. I was thankful we never had to take the bus because we had a car. We did use the bus as a resource because we could give the driver books that needed to be dropped off in the outer regions. There was a well-used path from our school store to the buses. Serving in such a remote area meant that we had to learn how to creatively use the resources we had.

Rusape was the gateway to the eastern highlands of Rhodesia. Rusape had Anglican, Roman Catholic, Methodist and Dutch Reformed church buildings in the town. It was a divided community, so these buildings were for the use of the Europeans. The local organizations were the Garden Club, Headlands Farm Association, Islamic Society, Lions Club, and Makoni Lodge of Free Masons, Makoni Farmers Association, Rusape Theatre Club, Rusape Round Table, Riding Club, and Women's Institute, all for the European population.

Our appointment in 1959 was two-fold. We were given the responsibility for conducting European worship services in English in Rusape. We worshipped in a small, rented building, the Women's Institute, while the congregation collected enough money to build a church. These services had been conducted by the pastor appointed to St. Andrew's in Umtali which was sixty miles away. The minister made the round trip from Umtali to Rusape two times per month. We would now be able to provide consistent worship for our town. Alec had a supervisory position over the African, native pastors who preached in the African churches. Alec did not preach routinely in the African churches. Sometimes he would be invited to speak at special events. At that time, Rhodesia had a total population of 6,207,300. Of this total 64% were Black and the white population was 35%, the colored (mixed) and the Asians were less than 1%. Ours was a rare privilege because we served a segment of that sharply divided white and black population living in the Rusape area, we were the only missionaries of the American Methodist Church appointed in Rusape. We were living in a house that belonged to the American branch of the Methodist Church working in Rhodesia at the time. It was a block house that was very modern for that era. It was relatively new and very nice. Luckily, the water to the house came from town so we did not have to boil it. We were fortunate to get two black and brown dachshunds for pets.

Dot in a very modern kitchen in the parsonage in Rusape

The house had a very large cypress hedge and a fence around the plot. The hedge was allowed to grow very tall. This tall growth meant that at Christmas we could cut the tops of the trees to be used for Christmas trees. The plot next door and at the back had very tall savannah grass which meant we had an abundance of snakes and small animals looking for food.

Alec, Dot, Karen, and Lex in front of the parsonage at Rusape

Our church in Rusape kept our American Methodist Church in Rhodesia multi-racial by serving both Europeans and Africans; however, this did not keep us from being misunderstood by both people groups. There were other branches of the Methodist Church working in the country at the time especially large numbers of the British Methodist Church. We had been assigned by Bishop Ralph Dodge to the work in Rusape under the Methodist Church from United States as missionaries. The World Division of the Board of Missions with headquarters in New York City was responsible for our salary as it was given through supporting churches in the USA.

In 1959 and early 1960 the Bishop appointed Alec to assist the African Church District Superintendent with the supervision of the churches in this area, but at conference in 1960 the districts were reorganized giving the Church District Superintendents full time appointments instead of combining the appointment with other work.

From that time, we had no responsibility for African Churches which came under our District Superintendent.

On arrival in Rusape we started weekly European church services, having an attendance of about 20 at each service. Literally and figuratively, we had set this little town of Rusape on FIRE. One day there was a fire burning the tall savannah grass from the back of our house to the main road. Every person within eyesight of the blaze or within smell of the fire came running. We begin to beat the fire down. The people were rewarded for their work by catching the small game running from the fire to have them for a meal. The town fire truck came with a source of water for putting out the remaining flames.

Nothing put the flames out in my body for I had started the fire by burning trash in a large barrel on the back of our lot. I was new to Rusape, new to the potential of the tall grass to become so dangerous with just one spark carried by the wind from the barrel. A young 21-year-old anxious to learn had stumbled upon a great truth, how great a forest is set ablaze by one spark. The tongue is written as fire in the scripture: James 3:5-6, So *also the tongue is a small member, yet it boasts of great exploits. How great a forest is set ablaze by a small fire! And the tongue is a fire. The tongue is placed among our members as a world of iniquity; it stains the whole body, sets on fire the cycle of nature.* (NRSV) and this too became very real to me. We were assigned to serve in this town with its people so divided. We were to work between the sharp knives of segregation and mistrust.

After a few months into the work two men on our plot brought out their knives at the door of our house ready to fight. I found myself between these two tribal enemies with tempers flaring, knives drawn. One of the worst things was that I knew them personally because they worked at the house. Matthew and Banai lived in the mission house.

Matthew worked in the house and Banai worked in the yard. They had seen our Christian work and we had hoped that our acts of faith would have made a difference in their lives. Instead, here they were screaming threats and brandishing weapons. My presence and the door of the house prevented them from striking. By standing between the two tribal rivals was the only way to stop the fight. I prayed that would work until I could close the door between the rivals. My screams brought help and the men were led away. Not only were we between the knives of many tribal groups but between the knives of the black and white of the area we had been appointed to serve. Standing between the knives of the two peoples we loved and had been appointed to serve meant we were often misunderstood and mistrusted by both communities.

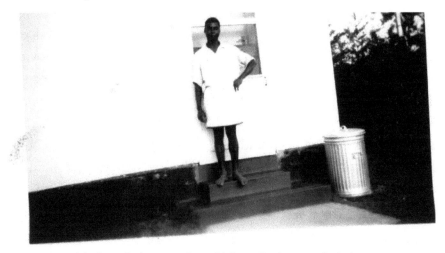

Matthew, the house worker, which put Dot between the knives

Many weeks later, when my labor started, I was doing mission work away from home. Alec had to drive me three hundred miles to get back to the hospital. The roads were bumpy and full of potholes. When I arrived at the European hospital in Rusape, the midwife gave me a washcloth to chew on when the contractions became intense. On

October 9th, the baby was born, and I remembered that faithful mother back in Pennsylvania. We named our daughter Karen Faith. It was government policy that ministers were not charged for medical services. I remained in the hospital eleven days without cost. During that time, representatives from the African hospital came to ask if I would donate some of my milk to feed the children at the African hospital that were needing care. This was just one more way that God called me to be in mission for Him.

Three months after her birth we took Karen to St. Andrews Methodist Church in Umtali for baptism by the Rev. Omar. We were so grateful for her life because of the measles I had contracted in Pennsylvania. We found that she had no lasting issues from my sickness or the injection that I had to have.

One afternoon I took Karen out in the stroller for a walk and sleep. I sat on a cement retaining wall in front of our house, just enjoying the fresh air. While sitting there a huge, fat, long, black snake began slithering toward us along the cement wall on which I was sitting. It was a black mamba snake, and they were deadly. They are very aggressive, and I had been told they could and would chase people. They could go as fast as ten miles per hour. There was no antidote currently. One bite and the venom moves quickly throughout the body, paralyzing quickly, followed by death. I felt my body stiffen, my heart race, my palms got wet, my eyes fixed on the snake. My prayer lifted to God in stammers, "Help, Lord, Help Lord!" without a sound coming from my mouth. Frozen like a statue I watched as that snake slithered along the way it came, only a few feet from the door of the house. We were no longer in danger, and I thanked God for His hand of protection.

Shortly after that, I realized I was pregnant again. Our family was growing, or so we thought. We lost that baby when I was five months pregnant, and we grieved the loss of our second child. The mission work continued. I never once regretted being on the mission field. I never thought that if I had stayed in the United States, I would not have lost my baby. I knew I was called by God to be where I was at that time.

In June of 1960 we organized a church in Rusape with a membership of twenty-one. We worshipped in the Women's Institute Building. In 1961 we purchased two lots for the church at a cost of $2,800. By December 25, 1962, The Groundbreaking Service was held for the new Wesley Church to be built in Rusape. Work was begun on the church building which was opened for worship on Easter Day of 1963. There were thirty-eight charter members. The church building cost $18,000 including furnishings. Of the cost, $12,000 was borrowed from a Building Society. Not one cent was received from America for this work.

Women's Institute Building in Rusape

We started class meetings each Friday evening and had 10 who attended. Our ministry had grown as evidenced by the building of the church and the increase in membership. The things we considered most important are the occasions when a person has found Christ. We will always remember the great grandmother coming forward to join the church on profession of faith. We have seen the seed of life planted in many hearts and we have seen it grow, thanks be to God!

During the time of church building and growing, in 1962, before the new church building was completed, Lee Alexander was born at the same hospital in Rusape where Karen had been born. When I arrived at the hospital in labor, the obstetrician told me to hurry up and deliver the baby. The doctor told me he was hungry and needed lunch. Even with that, the baby we called Lex was safely born. He was baptized by Rev. Tom Curtis in the Women's Institute Building where we were conducting weekly services before the new church opened.

The builder of the church, George Van Rensburg, requested to be the first person baptized in the new building after he had used his skills to build it. He had found God as he put the building together, never having given his heart to the Lord and having constructed a house of worship was a God experience for him. We used the town swimming pool for baptism because our members wished to be immersed. Our faithful musician was Joy Vermaak. She had five girls, and her husband was Bertie, a man who was a painter and dependent on alcohol. At the age of 42, he died and was buried in the town cemetery. Joy wore very high heel shoes that needed to have the heels covered. The heels left their imprint everywhere Joy walked in the church on the new floor. It was Joy's elder girl that received the first ever Crusade Scholarship in this community of Europeans.

One sad commentary is that in 1962 one church and two classroom blocks used for church services were burned during political unrest. In 1963 Magura church was burned. They were all in the area of our work. It is sad that the church, which supported African aspirations for independence, suffered this destruction.

In the area where we worked during our first term there were five African pastors serving five circuits. Some circuits have as many as twenty preaching places. When they arrived in one of their assigned places, they would preach for several days and then move to another place. These pastors used bicycles and public buses for transportation. The bicycle was sometimes transported on top of the bus to the area where the pastor would work.

Muziti was our largest school situated at the base of a large granite mountain. The church at Muziti was served by Rev. John Nemaungwe, a father of six with big dreams. He talked of going into business. He dreamed of going to University. His actions kept pace with his dreams. When the offering plate was passed, he put himself in the plate saying to all in the service "I Give My Self." This devout servant of God and many others like him were responsible for the tremendous growth of the church in Africa. Alec buried John's first-born child at Muziti and later buried Pastor John as he was killed on his motor bike at Headlands while taking the saving message of God's love to his parish. What an unbearable sadness!!

Wesley United Methodist Church in Rusape

Chapter Seven: Schools

It was He who gave gifts to people he appointed some to be apostles, others to be prophets, others to be evangelists, others to be pastors and teachers. Ephesians 4:11 (GNTD)

The other part of our assignment was to manage the schools. In 1959, our school district was the Chiduku-Chikore District Schools; it consisted of fifteen schools with 75 native teachers and about 2,700 children. The schools were Arnoldine, Chigora, Chigudu, Chikore, Chinyadza, Chitenderano, Chizawana, Dewerwi, Gurure, Macheke, Muziti, Magura, Rukweza, Sharara and Zambuko. There was only one school which went as high as the 8th grade. The remaining fourteen went only to the fifth grade.

The native teachers were trained in a Teacher Training School sponsored by the church. There were six sites but none that were managed by Alec. Once they finished the Training School and were hired by Alec in the District, my job was to sit through their classes to watch their performance. They taught the usual subjects: math, science, history, and grammar. All classes were taught in English. Students would come from different areas of the region and not all spoke the same dialect. So, teaching in English was a leveling agent. However, during recess, the kids spoke their native language while playing. But as soon as they came back in the classroom, they would easily revert to speaking English.

As I sat through all the different classes for the teachers, I had to complete long paper reports about their abilities to teach the subject and manage the class. If someone did not pass the standard, they were removed as a teacher at the school. There were seventy-five teachers to evaluate routinely and that kept me busy. Unfortunately, some had to be removed because they became involved with alcohol or drugs. One of the benefits of being a teacher in the district was that teachers were given a house on the mission property. As long as they stayed credentialed and in good standing, the house was theirs to use.

While I was busy evaluating the teachers at the different schools, I had help with watching Karen back at home. We lived 105 miles from Salisbury where Granny Alvord, Alec's mom, lived and we often had her visit. She would drive herself to Rusape and stay for a month at a time. During these times it was always wonderful to have another set of hands to help. I got along well with my mother-in-law. She was much older than I was, and I learned so much from her. During these times, while I was working in the schools, Karen had the benefit of being cared for by her granny.

Alec was responsible for paying the teacher salaries and keeping the schools supplied and maintained. In Rhodesia, children in primary and secondary schools had to pay to attend. College fees were free for qualified children. Parents would do whatever they could to pay the school fees. Sometimes they would barter with cows or goats to get their children a place in the school because they knew that an education was priceless.

Places in school were such a premium. There were never enough places for the qualified students. Alec prepared a test to try and be as fair as he could to all students. Only two students from each of our fifteen schools could go on to the Upper Primary School. One mother chewed the bark from the tree, a time-consuming work, to make a rug. She came into our house and knelt on the floor before Alec pleading for a place in school for her son Daniel. He was well qualified to go

45

to Upper Primary School (5th grade), but he was not one of the two students we could send. It was very hurtful to be put in this kind of position with the people we loved and were there to serve. Trying to be a representative of Christ and making these decisions that were limiting and excluding well qualified children from an education created that feeling of being between the knives. Alec did buy the rug hoping the mother could use the funds to search for a school for Daniel.

One of the classes in the school. These children were able to afford to attend school.

We had two students who borrowed a boat to cross the swollen river between Dewerwi and Chikore schools. They drowned trying to claim their places in the Upper Primary School. Education meant so very much and the children were willing to sacrifice their life to attain it.

In January 1960, tragedy struck at Arnoldine School, about an hour's drive from Rusape. Oliver Kamasoko was the Headmaster at Arnoldine. Oliver and Dorothy, his wife, had had a two-year-old child and she was pregnant with their second child. Dorothy, also a teacher, was pressing clothes under the thatched roof overhang of their house with a charcoal iron; Oliver was nearby using benzene to clean a pair of trousers. The benzene ignited and the thatched roof caught fire. Oliver and Dorothy were seriously burned. The house was completely destroyed. The two-year-old child was saved. Dorothy and Oliver were taken to the African hospital in Rusape. The police called our house asking for Alec to go to the house to collect the cash box containing all the school funds and important records. While he was gone to the house the hospital called asking for him to come to the hospital. Dorothy lost the baby she was carrying and had lost so much fluid she was near death. They were requesting a pastor. I told the nurse on the telephone that Alec had gone to Arnoldine to collect the strong box. The nurse said, "Well, you come and come now, or there will be no need to come."

Karen was just three months old; I knelt down by the cot and asked God to look after my baby. I grabbed my straw hat and ran out the back to the main road. I hitched a ride, for the first time in my life, to the African hospital in the center of the town. I got there in time to pray with Dorothy and Oliver. They accepted Christ and Dorothy went on to glory as I prayed. Little did I realize I had been gone from home for more than two hours. I became concerned for my own baby. The nurse loaned me her English style bike with the brakes on the handlebars. I started home riding that bicycle. Back in the United States growing up, I had ridden only a bike with back pedal brakes.

While riding home from the hospital I hit deep sand in a curve in the road. When I applied the brakes, the front brakes caught, and I landed in a six-foot ditch. My hat crushed, my leg cut, my arm broken. I got up and, on that bike, again. God only knows how I made it. I got home to find my baby gone. A neighbor had come to get my baby. The gardener had gone to get the neighbor when he saw me leaving the house with my hat on and running to the main road without the baby. I ended up in the African hospital that I had just left. This hospital had an x-ray machine, and the European hospital did not. For a long six weeks I could not completely care for Karen. After Dorothy's death, Oliver lost his will to live, and Alec was with him when he died. Their surviving two years old child went to the care of extended family members

We had an Opal station wagon loaded to visit schools, sometimes staying at a school for a week at a time. On one occasion we were going to visit Dewerwi. I packed the cloth diapers (there were no disposable diapers in Africa at that time) and all the things needed to care for a baby. The roads were badly washed in places and the ruts were deep, leaving a high center in the middle of the road. Alec hit a rock and broke off the drainage plug under the gas tank. He crawled under the car to put his hand over the hole to save our gas. He shouted to me," Get something to plug up this hole." It was my "Sunlight soap" that proved to be useful. Sunlight soap came in large, long chunks that you would cut to the size you needed to do laundry or bathe or do the dishes. It was made with lye and lard. It also was used in plugging the hole long enough for us to get back to the main highway for repairs. Otherwise, it would have been a three day wait for a public bus. With all of these issues, thank goodness the baby was being breast-fed. One less issue to worry about.

On another occasion we were staying the night in a tent without a floor. We made our bed on the ground just as it was getting dark. We were using a kerosene lantern. I picked up the quilt one last time to straighten out the wrinkles and discovered it was covered with small scorpions. We slept in the car! Consequently, we purchased a VW Westphalia Camper which made our school visits much easier.

It was on one of these school visits when we stopped to fill the tank with gas that we permitted Karen to stretch her legs. A large dog like a Rhodesian ridgeback bit her in the face creating a fear within her for many years and forever marking her face with scars.

Once when Alec was away visiting schools, I had a terrible fright. The two children were small. It was night and someone broke a window in the guest room. When I turned on the light in the room the screen was up, and a foot was protruding into the room. The foot quickly withdrew when I turned on the light. When I turned off the light the foot protruded through the window once more. I ran to the telephone and called for help. Neighbors came to my rescue.

When the district was moved to new leadership led by African nationals at the end of 1963 there were 17 schools, 100 teachers and about 3,500 children in the district. Two new schools, Nemanje and Nyahowe were added to Alec's responsibility. In addition, three schools had grade classes first through eighth grade, and one school went through seventh grade. Under our management thirty-three new teacher's houses had been built, 10 teachers houses had been improved, 42 new classrooms had been built, 18 classrooms had been improved. Alec enjoyed construction and had the privilege to see one new church building built at Chigora School and two new parsonages, one at Chitenderano School, and one for the African pastor in Rusape. Alec had a hobby of drawing plans, a hobby that benefited many of our schools and churches. He drew all the plans for the teachers' houses, but the classrooms and churches were built following an approved conference plan.

The seventeen schools in the Chiduku-Chikore District were reassigned from us in January 1964 to Mr. Gumbedza, who was appointed as School Manager. We were given seven other schools south of Umtali. These seven schools had fifty-one teachers and 1,800 children. When we began our work in 1959, there was only one African School Manager. Gradually, missionaries were replaced by Africans and Alec was the last missionary School Manager in the Methodist Church.

Chapter Nine: Vacation Travel

Six days you shall labor, but on the seventh day you shall rest; even during the plowing season and harvest you must rest. Exodus 34:21 (NIV)

Our Missionary Handbook stated that it was healthy to have a time away from the assignment. A travel allowance was provided if you gave proof of vacation time. When Alec was younger and on a flight, there was a medical emergency on the plane. The pilot saw on the manifest that there was a doctor on the plane. When the passenger verified that he was in fact a doctor, the pilot asked for his help. The doctor refused and stated he was on vacation. That made a tremendous impact on Alec and often factored in when we discussed vacation. Alec did not want to be known as someone who did not help when asked.

We had experienced illness from visits to schools in the lowland where it was hot, and mosquitoes were prevalent. Karen had many bouts of malaria in her young life. Since we had so much illness that took us away from the mission, we often did not take additional time away for vacation. In 1962 we went to Inyanga, Rest Haven for vacation. During that time, Alec worked to get the mission books and reports ready for audit. He said that the only way he was going to get the books done was to find some time away from the mission. Another time that year Lex was hospitalized in Salisbury, and we were away from the mission.

In 1963, as we approached the end of our first five years term in missions, we finally did get some true time away and went to South

Africa. The Board of Missions paid for us to have a three-week vacation. We traveled by car by way of Biet Bridge, Transvaal, Natal, Cape Town, and Orange Free State. We were tracing memories for Alec as he had vacationed there with his parents while he was growing up.

Other than that trip, I was often treated with some mini vacations each time Alec went to Salisbury to meet with the Bishop. He would work and I got to rest at Mom Alvord's house. After Alec's parents retired from mission work in Rhodesia, they built a house in Salisbury in 1936. It was a large house because they had a large family, and they had a pool in the back. The family all called it the Big House. Mom Alvord had hired several servants who were nationals to provide jobs for the Africans. When I visited, each meal felt like I was eating at a restaurant. As the children got older, they enjoyed the pool.

Chapter Ten: Winds of Change-Missionary Go Home

Who is like the wise? Who knows the explanation of things? A person's wisdom brightens their face and changes its hard appearance. Ecclesiastes 8:1 (NIV)

MY AFRICA

Glittering and colored flowers over plains and hills,
Way down below the hill's valley still,
Happy and singing birds shrill.
Up in the clothed trees.
All is found in this land of my fathers.
But all is brought and owned by others.

What puts my native land behind?
To other lands it is not bound.
Much and much more it receives
But little, even, even little it still gives.
Many people have done great deeds.
But more of its own it still needs

Many Martyrs have themselves sacrificed for it.
Many people from a far have improved it.
But for its own leaders still it clamors.
Clamoring for leaders with God's whole armor.
Leaders from within its bounds.

Blessings have over it showered.
But still more of its own it aspires.
Its own to others have wisdom not showed.
Give a hand to our desperate continent
And abstain from human selfishness!
Don't rest in mean ides content
But grow in forms of helpfulness.

Africa is an eagle of the upper sky.
To the chicken it has been eluded.
It is as beautiful as lands you ever spied.
Black and white piano keys should be included
To produce harmonious music to all
And grant equality to all.
Africa, fly on until you reach the upper sky!

Our friend Marjorie Smock let us use the creative work of one of her students, Mutero Chihuri, to express the desire of the young in our schools for freedom, for pride in their country, and for something of their own!

The African continent was in upheaval with twenty-five countries gaining independence during the 1950's and 1960's and the names of countries were changed to reflect the new freedoms. Countries fighting for independence saw what had happened in the Belgium Congo when 100,000 people died in the civil war. The white minority in Southern Rhodesia worried. Between 1953 and 1963 Southern Rhodesia joined with Northern Rhodesia and Nyasaland to create the Federation of Rhodesia and Nyasaland. This lasted only a short time because the winds of change were blowing all over the continent. Northern Rhodesia broke the Federation and changed its name to Zambia. In the late 1960's Rhodesia and South Africa were the only countries that were still independent states governed by a white minority with European descent and culture. The white minority who was in power in the government declared a Unilateral Declaration of Independence and became known simply as Rhodesia. However, the two African Nationalist parties in Rhodesia led an armed insurgency and a civil war started. There were factions within the white government that championed a more diverse government but with the requirement that the local Africans obtained a higher education. During the initial phases of the civil war, most white citizens carried personal weapons and sometimes white housewives even carried submachine guns. All civilian transport had to be escorted in convoys for safety. It was not unusual to hear about rural farms and villages being attacked by guerrillas.

All this time, we were caught in the middle of the political tensions, even though we were not in the main urban areas of the country. Churches established by missionaries were then expected to provide a new kind of servant leadership from the missionaries. Some even called for a moratorium, believing the Africans had to flex their muscles without the aid of western leadership.

In this climate of change new strategies and direction along with dynamic leadership was needed. Our Bishop Ralph E. Dodge wrote a book entitled Unpopular Missionary, subtitled Missionary Go Home! Published by Harper and Brothers, New York. If the mission was to expand, it needed aggressive recruitment that would attract the right quality of young missionaries. We saw a large number of missionaries that began to go home.

In Birmingham, Alabama at this time four little African American girls Denise McNair, Cynthia Wesley, Carole Robertson, and Addie Mae Collins were killed by a bomb in the Eleventh Avenue Baptist Church while attending Sunday School. This was hot news on the front pages of the paper in Rhodesia. The people we were working with had many questions for me about segregation in my own home state. Many comparisons were made about the separation of peoples in the United States and what we were doing as a church in Africa where our church served both peoples separately. Our work was again between the knives. Ecclesiastes 11:1 became an important verse, *Ship your grain across the sea; after many days you may receive a return.* By sending missionaries, and learning about peoples of diverse cultures, tolerance and a desire for equality returned to feed those working for equal rights in the United States. It was so very important what happened in the United States because other countries were watching what we are doing. When we have sent our citizens to work in other countries for justice and there is no justice at home then our message is questioned by the people we came to serve. O: Lord we see the truth of the statement "Mission is from everywhere to everywhere."

We had just finished our first term and were returning to the United States. Dr. and Mrs. Emmett Johnson, professors from Emory University in Atlanta, Georgia, replaced us in Rusape to serve Wesley Church. The Bishop visited us just before we left Rusape and his message in his book caused us to ask many questions and influenced the way we packed our bags to go home perhaps not to return. It was hard but we had to leave our dachshunds behind. A family in Rusape took them since we could not take the dogs with us. We had had them for the entire five years and we were leaving a part of our family behind. As we packed our bags, we remembered, "Whatever happens our confidence as children of God is that all things work together for good to them that love God."

In the country at the time of our leaving all School Managers in our denomination were African nationals. The missionary was no longer appointed for that work; we were the last missionary with that appointment. We had achieved a very important part of the work that we were assigned to do.

Part III: Pinnacle, A View of the Mountain

But they that wait for the Lord shall renew their strength; they shall mount up with wings as eagles; they shall run, and not be weary; they shall walk and not faint." –

Isaiah 40:31 (RSV)

Chapter Eleven: First Furlough

When his time of service was completed, he returned home. Luke 1:23 (NIV)

On May 17, 1964, we began our 5,838 miles from Rhodesia to the United States. Our first term of service as missionaries was completed. We first took a train 240 miles to the Mozambique coastal town of Beira where we would board the ship, Bramer Castle. As the train traveled through Mozambique, hordes of children stood on the side of the tracks where the train stopped. They were scantily clothed and had signs of malnutrition. They were begging for anything to be given to them. We had so much, and I just started opening the suitcases we had with us and threw whatever I could. Lex was upset when I started throwing his personal items out the window. It was hard to explain to a 2-year-old why I was doing what I was doing.

We planned a three-month driving trip through Europe and our VW Westphalia Camper vehicle was going with us on the train and then on the ship. But first, we had stops in Dar-es-Salaam and Zanzibar in Tanzania. The ship was a passenger ship, and we enjoyed the ability to be able to be on deck and have activities to do.

When we reached Mombassa, Kenya, our two children were joined on the ship with over 200 other children that were refugees from Kenya to escape the horrific political situation. The Mau uprising in Kenya reflected a lot of the same issues that were going on in Rhodesia. Loss of land to white settlers, poverty, and lack of true political representation for Africans only fueled the revolt. The Kenyan children on the ship were the lucky ones that were escaping the carnage. They were being relocated to countries all over the world. But they were leaving their families behind, families that they probably would never see again. It was not long after the Kenyan children coming aboard that mumps broke out on the ship.

The ship made steady progress with stops in Aden in Yemen and finally Suez in Egypt. Alec left the ship in Suez so that he could take a side trip to some sites with special significance in the Old Testament. He was taking advantage of an educational agenda to Cairo. The children and I could not go with him because of the mumps outbreak. Karen and Lex were quarantined, even though they did not have an active case of mumps. So, we enjoyed the adventure of going through the Suez Canal. Alec joined the ship in Port Said in Egypt and the trip across the Mediterranean carried on. We disembarked in Italy, with two children who then had an active case of mumps.

From Italy we started the journey through Europe. We drove all through Italy, Switzerland, Lichtenstein, Austria, Germany, France, Belgium, Netherlands, crossed the channel to England then to Denmark, Sweden, and Norway. Before I had left Rhodesia, I was able to find some inexpensive cotton at 10 cents per yard. I made extra thick padding from the cotton to make some pull up underwear for the children. At every stop I located a sink to wash the underwear. Because they were cotton, they also dried very quickly. I did not have a dryer to throw the clothes in to dry. It seemed like I had made a lot of underwear and I washed a lot of underwear. I was thankful that I had prepared to do this because we had a lot of Europe to cover in a short period of time.

Alec loved to collect coins and paper money from all over the world. This driving trip gave him such a wonderful opportunity to enjoy his hobby. He made sure to exchange money in each country. The VW Westphalia Camper was our home as we camped in it for those three months. Soon it was time to board another ship and head to the United States. This trip went from Norway to the United States and took weeks. Another chapter in our lives at sea.

We left the ship in New York and collected our faithful traveling home, our VW Westphalia Camper. Our first stop, on August 23, 1964, was in Wetona and Big Pond, Pennsylvania, the place we had left so quickly five years earlier, heading to Rhodesia. It felt like we had never left. The people of the church, some of them were there five years earlier and helped us to pack in a 24-hour period, welcomed us back with love and joy. The welcome was almost overwhelming. The first time I had come to this home I was a newlywed wife. We left a family of two. Now I was still a wife but also a mother and a world traveler. And they welcomed a family of four back home.

We begin a time of waiting on the Lord to show us what was to be next in our service. Would we return to Rhodesia? In the waiting time we were still serving and studying to show ourselves approved. We had been granted a study leave from the Board of Missions for two years.

We moved on after our welcome home by the churches we served in 1958 to 1959. Our next trip took us to Birmingham, Alabama. The children and I remained with my parents. Alec went to Duke University in Durham, North Carolina to work on his Master of Theology. I kept a full schedule of speaking engagements the three months we were in Alabama. Sometimes I went to the speaking engagement by borrowing a car or renting a car. Sometimes I used public transport or my parent's car. I even hired a taxi at times.

While I was fulfilling the requirement to serve the churches who had sponsored us while in Rhodesia, my mother cared for Karen and Lex. She and my dad loved having their grandchildren living with them. My parents thoroughly spoiled them. My mother let them do what they wanted, and Karen and Lex loved being with my parents.

On the weekends when Alec could come to Alabama, we continued to honor speaking engagements at the churches in Birmingham. During our visits to the sponsoring churches, I received a lot of United Methodist Women's Mission Recognition pins.

From September to June Alec did field work in the Western North Carolina Conference on the Surry Circuit. He met Dr. Frank Jordan, the District Superintendent, who shared that one of his ministers, Ross Francisco was ill and needed help with his appointment. The responsibility was two small churches near the Virginia State Line, Epworth, and Zion.

The children and I moved to Durham in January of 1965 to be with Alec. We lived at the Worm Ranch until June 1965. This "Ranch" sold fishing worms as well as rented out small houses. We did not have a lot of furniture. I put a mattress on top of our travel trunks that became the beds where the children slept.

We traveled each weekend to the Surry Circuit and stayed in a motel with Alec. Alec would visit the members of the church and on Sundays he would preach. Sometimes we went with him to the different churches. Sometimes we stayed either in Durham or in the motel near the churches. When I stayed in Durham I sewed for family. I could not work outside the home because we only had one vehicle and no available childcare. I found a place where I could get fabric for 30 to 50 cents per yard. I would make Alec a vest and I would make myself a matching skirt. I did not own a sewing machine, so I rented a Singer sewing machine.

In March 1965, Dr. Frank Jordan asked Alec if he would like an appointment in the Western North Carolina Conference. We did not know if we would be needed in Rhodesia as the civil war for independence was going on. Alec told him that he would like an appointment at conference time, June 1965. Alec changed his conference membership from the Rhodesian Annual Conference to the Western North Carolina Conference.

On June 24, 1965, we moved to the Pinnacle Charge in the Winston-Salem District to serve Pinnacle, Chestnut Grove, and Mt. Zion Churches. The next day the foundation was poured for a new church at Pinnacle. Pinnacle was the nearest community to Pilot Mountain, a natural icon in North Carolina. The church was located in sight of that picturesque mountain. Excitement flooded our being; building was so very much a part of Alec's ministry. I knew we would be there until that building was completed.

Alec preached at 9:00am at Pinnacle, 10:00am at Chestnut Grove and 11:00am at Mt. Zion each Sunday. It was not unheard of for him to preach at a 2:00pm District Meeting and then hold a Bible Study that night. God had called him to preach, and this was feeding his soul, even more than Rhodesia where the work was primarily schoolwork. Educational work was my calling. Alec's preaching skills were being honed as he always had his spiritual life enhanced by Dr. Stephen Olford on the radio. Sometimes the children and I went with him to some of the services. We would wait for him on the highway for him to pick us up as he drove from one church to another one. The children became used to attending the different churches, which were quite unique from each other. Some churches were older people and other churches had younger families. We met a very congenial and loving person at one of the churches who ended up being Karen's teacher at school. That was a red-letter day in our life when our first-born child Karen Faith started school at Pinnacle Elementary in Stokes County with Miss Jones as her teacher. I had the opportunity to begin substituting in the school system at that time. Lex was too young to begin preschool and he was taken care of by a church member.

The parsonage was old and very run down. The church needed a new parsonage badly. The paint on the old rigid boards were crackling off. We painted the stairwell because it was so bad. One good thing was that at the back of the house was a field for a vegetable garden. As we served there, we realized the mission homes in Rhodesia were in much better shape compared to the home we now occupied. The larger of the churches we currently served was in debt for the church building, with nothing left over for the parsonage. We managed to continue to serve in this mission field.

Mom Alvord traveled alone by plane from Rhodesia to the United States in 1965. She came to Alec's graduation from Duke in June and remained in the states visiting her family and missionary friends. She came back to our house in Pinnacle to celebrate her 74th birthday on November 19. The year, 1965, we traded our faithful camper, that we had used for so many miles in Europe and the United States. It had become unreliable and with the churches that Alec served, we needed something dependable. We got a good trade on the camper and Alec got a nice little sports car. He paid $900 for the car, a Carman Ghia two-seater that got great gas mileage. Thankfully, the kids were small enough to fit in the back when all four of us needed to go somewhere. So, we managed in our new little car and Alec got to drive a sports car.

Parsonage at Pinnacle, NC with Alec's little sports car

When Mom Alvord left on November 30, Alec drove her in his new car to New York. Mom Alvord boarded the Queen Mary ocean liner for her trip back to Africa. Mom Alvord had told us that she wanted to die in Africa and have her remains left there. Alec's dad, Emory, was already buried at Waddilove a British Methodist Mission Station where they were working in retirement to get the mission out of debt. We wondered if this would happen before we saw her, alive, again.

The next year, 1966 spring semester, Alec began classes in French and German at Wake Forest to enhance his study of the Old Testament. He wanted to be able to read original manuscripts that read other people's interpretation of the Holy Bible. During this time, he continued to preach multiple services each Sunday. On May 19, 1966, just a year after we started our appointment at the charge, an Open House was held at the new Pinnacle Church. For the next year, we just lived life. Alec served the churches, I substitute taught at the schools, Karen went to school and Lex was cared for by a caring church member.

In March 1967, the children and I went back to Alabama. I was invited to speak at the Annual Meeting of the Women's Society of Christian Service (WSCS) of the North Alabama Conference with the theme "We Commit Ourselves Anew." The scripture "Commit thy way unto the Lord; trust also in Him; and He shall bring it to pass." Psalms 37:5 (KJV) was the focus. I could see God's plan for us in the invitation.

"We invoke the Spirit of God in our midst this hour,
As a symbol of His presence, we light the Master candle,
Our hearts the altar and His love the flame.
In the white light of God's love
The darkness of our lives stands out in bold relief—
The selfishness, the smallness, the resentments, the secret sins.

Shall we not commit ourselves anew?
Surrendering our all that His light may shine in us?
These other candles represent our commitment
All that we may grow in understanding and spiritual power.
That we may increase our knowledge of the needs of the world.
And share through witness and service in the outreach of the church.
God, we pray Thee, let your light shine through the
Woman's Society of Christian Service
In this North Alabama Conference."

This ceremony was followed by the hymn: "Take My Life." There I was committing myself anew to service, but the path of service was not clear. We were serving in Pinnacle where Alec was finding fulfillment but still in deep concern for our people in Rhodesia. The fires of independence continued to ignite all over that land. And naturally we were also concerned about Alec's mother and siblings and their families that still lived in Rhodesia. We hoped they would remain safe.

I became pregnant in the fall of 1967 with the baby's due date on June 10, 1968. By the New Year's holiday, I was in the Forsyth Hospital, unable to carry the baby. It was just dreadful. We grieved the loss of our baby, and the pain was knife like. Luckily, we had a church member keep Karen and Lex while I was away. During this time, Alec was in correspondence with church leaders in Rhodesia. We were given the directive to return to Rhodesia after Alec finished his term of service with the Western North Carolina Annual Conference. In May 1968, the District Ministers gave a reception to all clergy leaving the Winston-Salem District. We were part of that reception. We were leaving the District heading back to Africa for a second term in Rhodesia.

We bought trunks from the neighborhood antique store. I painted the trucks black, and we were packed up by moving day in June. We began to visit in local churches, district meetings, jurisdictional and conference meetings sharing the mission story and our commitment to return to Africa. After we moved out of the parsonage, we traveled to Birmingham, Alabama. We remained in Birmingham with my parents until our departure for Africa. Alec had to be in Rhodesia by December 10th and left before me and the children. I took the children by myself for a later flight. We traveled to Rhodesia by plane via New

67

York, London, Rome, Johannesburg, and Salisbury, the capital city of Rhodesia. We were greeted by all of Alec's family for a family reunion at the Big House. We were finally home again.

Part IV: Murewa,

The Big Elephant

And I tell you that you are Peter, and on this rock, I will build my
church, and the gates of Hades will not overcome it.

Matthew 16:18b (NIV)

Chapter Twelve: Second Term of Service

And now, Israel, what does the Lord your God ask of you but to fear the Lord your God, to walk in obedience to him, to love him, to serve the Lord your God with all your heart and with all your soul. Deuteronomy 10:12 (NIV)

In 1909, Dr Samuel Gurney set his eyes north in Rhodesia. He had heard of a large area which, yet had been closed to the Christian Gospel. Persistent as always in his work for the Kingdom, he set out to break the barrier for his Lord. He was not wanted and not welcomed.

On arriving at Murewa, Dr. Gurney was told by the local District Commissioner that so far, the district had been spared two evils, cattle sickness, and missionaries. To put it bluntly, there was no place for him in the district so he may as well go back from where he had come, back to Old Umtali Mission. Not satisfied with the word of the District Commissioner, Dr Gurney decided to see the local Chiefs. Again, he found that he was not wanted and not welcome.

How could these barriers of suspicion and dislike be broken? He had an idea. He had another vocation. There was no medical doctor in the area. Though not welcome as a missionary, he was welcomed as a doctor.

The children in a nearby village were teasing some cattle. The bull gored one of the little girls across the stomach, her intestines were hanging out. The children called her parents, and her father was the local chief. He remembered Dr. Gurney had said he was a doctor. The chief sent for Dr. Gurney. He quickly came to see the little girl. Dr. Gurney washed the intestines of the child and since they were not broken, he put them back in her stomach and stitched her up. That opened the way for Dr. Gurney and the work of missions in that area. The barriers were broken slowly with his medical skills. He knew things were going to work out when he was given approval to build a clinic. Dr. Gurney was told he could build only one room, so he cleverly built it very large so he could partition the inside. A mission site was granted, a clinic opened and then a school. Job Tsiga was the first teacher and Murewa Methodist Centre was founded by these two servants of God.

Dr. Gurney and Job Tsiga moved on to open new work at Nyadiri. Others followed in their steps, building on the solid foundation which has been laid for us on the solid rock, Christ our Lord. Nyadiri was twenty-five miles up the strip road from Murewa.

As one walks around Murewa one finds evidence of the past, including: the foundation of Dr. Gurney's first clinic. You can see graves for those who died in the 1918 flu epidemic. The building used over forty years ago as a dormitory can still be seen. Howard Memorial Church, which has been rebuilt twice on the same site, speaks of the faithful toil of those who have gone before. We were shown a picture of the child who had been gored by the bull. In the picture she was an eighty-year-old grandmother.

On the landscape at Murewa there is a huge granite mountain that bears the resemblance of an elephant. It is called Hurungwe. Nearby was another granite mountain called Zhongwe and there are seven smaller granite outcrops around it. One of the many stories told by the people of Hurungwe and Zhongwe was that the mountains had a fight and Zhongwe was driven away Hurungwe kept Zhongwe's seven "wives," the smaller outcrops of granite.

Dot, Karen, and Lex with Hurungwe in the background.

Our second term of service and our appointment was to Murewa Mission Center as Principal of the schools. Murewa is a beautiful place. We considered it a great privilege to be appointed to serve as principal of this fine center with an enrollment of 820 students and a staff of 30 teachers in its two schools. What is our work here? The following questions and comments may give you a glimpse into our missions work.

- "A Bishop is visiting from America; can you entertain him for a few days?"

- "There are visitors from USA will you greet them at the gate?"

- "The gas line is leaking in my bathroom; can you fix it?"

- "The bull has just gored one of our oxen, what shall we do?"

- "Please hurry to the boys' boarding, there is a fight between two boys."

- "I have been called to a meeting; can you take the service tomorrow for me?"

- "The engine at the generator is making strange noises, come quickly!"

- "It was making noises--$1,500 worth of strange noises! "

- "The question is: where do we get the funds to repair it?"

- "We need a library!"

- "We need more classrooms!"

- "We need a larger office!"

- "We need a science lab!"

- "We need an assembly hall big enough to take our student body!"

- "Come quickly the boys were studying in the locker room with a candle and started a fire!"

- "The nurse is here, one of our students is very sick with malaria; we need transport to the hospital at Nyadiri."

- "The Magistrate has just had some of our students that were working on the property line arrested."

The voices cried incessantly. During all the confusion, Hurungwe, the granite elephant, stands above it all. He reminds us of the power of God who out of His great Love sent His only Son to bring PEACE to our hearts

During this time, the white European population of Rhodesia had sharpened anxiety about the possibility of African rule. The white government took the steps to unilaterally declare independence (UDI) from the British Commonwealth, but they did not do the work to establish majority rule. The whites were attempting to delay the transition of government to the Africans. The action was negatively viewed at the United Nations and the UN voted for economic sanctions against Rhodesia. That only hurt the Africans. The embargo meant the Rhodesian Forces were hampered by a lack of modern equipment but used other means to obtain war supplies. The white government acquired oil, munitions, and arms via the Apartheid government of South Africa. War material was also obtained through elaborate international smuggling schemes, domestic production, and equipment captured from infiltrating enemy combatants. All of this done to keep the civil war going, while the African citizens of the country suffered.

After UDI, the government led by Ian Smith enacted a long series of laws that transformed the country into a replica of her neighbor, the Republic of South Africa. For example, few multi-racial areas existed in the country. The Land Tenure Act defined black and white sectors and Africans were forcibly removed from choice land. Government aid of African education was proportionately less than the subsidy to white schools and then was further reduced. The main African political parties were banned, and African spokesmen continue to be harassed and jailed. But the political tensions weren't going to last. The African population was gradually making progress toward African rule. And Alec and I were helping to prepare the African people to be ready to rule.

The principal's house at Murewa faced this large elephant shaped mountain. Some mornings it looked like he winked as the sun rose to say. "Look I have been here from the beginning of time, and I will be here forever" a reminder God is always present in our everyday, watching over our coming in and our going out. Take heart nothing is going to happen to you that you and God cannot manage. We ate at the table Dr. Gurney brought to Murewa. The table was large enough for twelve people. It always remained in the principal's house because the house itself was large and the dining room was built to accommodate many guests. Since the principal's house was right at the gate of the Mission Center, we never knew when people would drop in for a meal or tea. I had a staff in the kitchen which helped to make sure we had tea items ready at all times. I learned quickly how to take a meal and stretch it to feed unexpected guests and we never wasted leftovers. Anything left over from a meal was the basis for another meal the next day. I became proficient in making leftovers taste like a new meal. We had a family code we used if there were more people at the table than we had food for, it was called FHB which meant "family hold back." That was the code used to take very small helpings of whatever was offered to ensure that our guests had plenty. We could always find something to eat after the meal if we were still hungry. Having kitchen help was both a blessing and a curse. Blessing because of having other hands to help. Curse were those same hands. I had a brand-new set of Teflon coated pots and pans. I was so excited to use them while preparing the meals. The women in the kitchen must have thought I was a terrible cook because the pots and pans were black inside. They were determined to give me a set of clean kitchenware to use. They took my new Teflon pots and pans outside and used sand to clean the black out. They were so proud, and it was excruciating to not cry when I saw how happy they were. I thanked them profusely in the work they had done.

One of the amazing stories of the mountain comes from our own family. In the early years of Alec's father's service, he climbed the mountain and attached a climbing cable to the top so that those who would come after could climb up more easily. Many people told the story in the following years about using the cable to get to the top.

"Build on the Rock" was the motto of the school. These both were literally and figuratively true. The buildings are built on rock which lies close to the surface wherever we dug. Our lives are built on Christ, the solid rock of our faith. During our two-year stay, a new dorm, library, staff houses, and office were built.

Our son Lex who was five years old at the time, had many friends his age, close to 20; they rode bikes about the center. They had a knack for finding the building sites and playing in the sand mounds the builders were planning to use. The boys would spread the sand all over the place and the building manager would come to me to complain. I often had to take away their bikes as a punishment. Then they found that the cattle troughs and even pig sties made a nice place for water play. One thing Lex did not enjoy was his visits next door to the clinic to see the nurse for his injections and treatment for worms and fungus on his head. The clinic was very close to our back door, and he had stood outside the door too much and watched what happened inside.

Murewa Mission Center Staff in 1969 consisted of a District Superintendent, District Schools Manager, Principal and Station Chairman. Alec was the Principal and Station Chairman. The Secondary School had twelve staff members. The Central Primary School Staff had eighteen members. District Administration had five staff members. All these persons needed accommodations for themselves and their families and that was the Station Chairman's responsibility. We needed to provide housing and all the amenities that the teaching and support staff needed.

It is the task of our teachers in the Primary and Secondary Schools to ensure that our students find the same firm foundation that we have all found in Christ. Children begin the first grade at Murewa, and some were able to complete Form IV or the twelfth grade. Both schools had full programs and we appreciated the time given so freely by all the staff. We were particularly appreciative of our Domestic Science teachers. In 1968, Murewa was the only school under the Division of African Education to take cookery as an examination subject for the Cambridge School Certificate. The school produced the food for our boarding students, using chickens, goats, pigs, cattle, vegetables, and fruit to supply a balanced diet. Cattle were a source of wealth. We had one student bring his only oxen to school to pay his school fees. This was an indication of how much value was placed on education.

In 1968 we had such a serious drought it looked as if the boarding schools would have to close. Parents were unable to pay school fees. A plan was devised to have parents come to school and build an amphitheater. The parents would pay their children's fees with their labor. That worked for a while but in the end, we were within a week of closing. We had dug pit latrines, rationed water, and did everything we knew to do to conserve. The leaders called for prayer day and night. After three days of prayer, it began to rain, our school did not close! God opened the heavens and blessed the land with rain.

For Karen and Lex, we had home school in a special room off our large, screened porch. There were government regulations preventing our children in attending the local school. If Karen or Lex went to the local school, it would take the place of an African child. In home school, we had formal lessons from 7-11 am. In the afternoon I went to the Secondary School to have class meetings with the senior girls. One of the schoolgirls would keep my children at home. One of the schoolboys would make a chip fire each afternoon in the boiler at the back of the house for hot water. We had electric lights from sundown till 10 pm thanks to the use of a generator. Sometimes the generator would not work, and we were left in the dark. We had to use candles for a little light. We had bottled gas for the fridge and for cooking.

Home School with Karen and Lex

Ours was a constant battle with scorpions and black ants in the house. The floors in part of the house were wide wooden planks with large cracks between the planks. We finally had to put the legs of the beds in jar lids of water to keep the ants off the bed. I had to inspect the clothes before they were laundered so that we would not get stung by a scorpion. We had mosquito nets for every bed as malaria was a constant. We praised God for the work that Dr. Gurney did and the hospital he established. We needed the hospital when I had a severe bout of malaria even though I was taking anti-malaria drugs. The mission hospital was a large African hospital in Nyadiri. I had to stay there for seven days while I took medications by mouth to get over the malaria. There were no private rooms, only large wards.

Nevertheless, it was an excellent hospital because the church was dedicated to the care of the African people. While I was in the hospital Mom Alvord came and helped Alec take care of the children.

While at Murewa, our second daughter and youngest child, Veranita Grace, was born April 1969. When labor started, we traveled to the hospital in Salisbury where she was born. Karen and Lex stayed with Alec's sister, Nancy, who also lived in Salisbury. When we were picking a name for our baby, I thought of Joy, the faithful musician at the church in Rusape. Her elder daughter was Veronica and that inspired us to name our baby. But we chose Veranita, meaning "little summer" in Spanish. When we brought the baby home from the hospital, Karen looked at Veranita and said very emphatically, "That is my baby." Karen truly cared for Veranita in all areas that a baby needed. When home school lessons started back for Karen and Lex, Veranita slept in the pram.

Christmas and Easter were very meaningful times at the mission center. The community gathered out on the rocks to enact the Christmas Story and afterwards the actors and the congregation proceeded around the community crying out in joy "Jesu wakababarwa" which means "Jesus was born." At Easter they started a march at sunrise through the community waving palm branches ending up at the rocks to relive the Easter story.

Our children were very comfortable with the language of their friends, and it was like turning on a light switch. When they were out to play it was Shona, when they entered the house, it was English. We had four high school teachers who had just returned from the United States and their children spoke English as a first language and found our children to be fast friends. Karen was in the scouting program with her friends. She had great fun cooking and sewing outside. She became very competent cooking over an open fire. It is interesting to learn that scouting was started in Rhodesia by Lord Baden Powell, a British general in the early 1900's and founded the modern Scouting movement.

Changes occurred for our denomination in 1968. Our church was now the United Methodist Church because of the union of the Methodist Church with the Evangelical United Brethren. The guidelines for missionary service had changed; a term was calculated in months. A term could be three years and a furlough three months. The term could be such that it considered the educational needs of the family. Work procedures on the mission field changed when the Boards of Mission of the two different church organization became one. What had been divisive became a uniting experience on the field.

History was also made in 1968 in the Methodist Church in Rhodesia with the election of the first African Bishop, The Rev. Abel Muzorewa. It was not a peaceful Annual Conference gathering. Hateful things were said to and about Bishop Muzorewa. Not all the people of the United Methodist Church in Rhodesia accepted him. We were privileged to be in attendance for that conference session when the program happened to be the 60th Anniversary of the Murewa Center.

We were also privileged to have the first African missionary of the Rhodesian Annual Conference on the staff at Murewa. Lydia Zimonte was Matron of the girls boarding. She was a strong leader of the Rukwadzano Women of Rhodesia (RRW). This group was similar to United Methodist Women in the United States. We had one hundred members, and it was a spiritually strong group. We met each Friday in the church. The pastor's wife, Renah Beulah Dikanifwa served as the president of the group. When we met, the women wore uniforms that were blue and red. Blue stood for the darkness that the women had been saved from. The red signified the blood of Jesus. The white on the duku, or the headdress, signified the Holy Spirit. The uniform had to be earned.

Rukwadzano Women of Rhodesia (RRW) in their uniforms.

Members could not drink beer or smoke. Members had to lead pious lives. Leaders would decide if a person had earned their uniform. Once the uniform was earned, people had to buy them and if someone could not afford it, they were still given a uniform paid by other people. Likewise, leaders could take uniforms away if a member started to have unchristian like behavior. If a uniform had been taken away, the person who used to wear the uniform could earn it back by showing they had returned to pious living. When members wore their uniforms in places outside of the church, they were respected. Secular people would call them "Jesus People." Often a woman wearing the uniform would get priority treatment; seated first at a dining room or on a bus. People knew the women wearing the uniform were doing good work for the people of Rhodesia. Other denominations, like the British Methodist, also had uniforms of different colors. I learned how to wear a duku at language school. Wearing the duku was a sign of respect. And the higher the duku the more elegant people thought you were. Wearing a duku was also very stylish. And a white duku was considered most holy.

During this time, the church began to plan for a nationwide revival. It was expected that people from all over Rhodesia would attend, which meant we had to be prepared for their spiritual and physical needs. Just outside of Salisbury, we began to put up straw huts for people to use during the one-week event. Alec and I also planned to run a store where people could come to get supplies that they needed while they were at the revival. The Annual Conference initially paid for the supplies and often we filled the van with things needed for the people. The money from the sale of supplies went back to the conference for reimbursement. After a month of planning, the day came for the revival to begin. Buses of people began to arrive. People came on foot or in vehicles or bicycles. Please came from all over Rhodesia. It was estimated that 11,000 people, men, women and children attended. The preaching, the singing and the praying was powerful. The Holy Spirit cut through the crowd and many who attended accepted Jesus as the Lord of their lives. A temporary baptistry was set up and many new disciples of Jesus were baptized. We saw firsthand the living definition of revival.

While the week was one of revival, we still had the day to day and sometimes the hour-by-hour responsibility of the store, and our own family. With that many people coming to the revival, it meant that our children had plenty of playmates. They stayed with us in close proximity to the store and enjoyed a week with no school or lessons.

Imagine what the people of Salisbury felt with having 11,000 African nationals descend on the city, even though it was not for political reasons but faith reasons. The country was divided and there were tensions. Rev. Nason Dikanifwa told the story of being questioned by a European policeman. In the course of the questions, he showed the officer the mark of the "M" on the palm of his hand, "See you bear the "tattoo" of God, I have it too, and we are all children of God." Even though they may have looked different, Rev. Difanifwa reminded the policeman that they both belonged to God. The policeman let him go. Rev. Dikanifwa also used everyday things in sermons. He used the making of bricks as an illustration. *As Christians we need to be like the burned brick. If we are burned by the Holy Spirit, we will stand up to the storms of life. If we do not have the Holy Spirit in our life, we will melt away like the sun-dried brick when the storms of life come to us.*

When the revival was over, people returned to their villages, again using buses, bikes, cars or on foot. God had used the time to sow seeds of faith and hope in the African people of Rhodesia.

Chapter Thirteen: Big Move

Instruct the wise and they will be wiser still; teach the righteous and they will add to their learning. The fear of the Lord is the beginning of wisdom, and knowledge of the Holy One is understanding. For through wisdom your days will be many, and years will be added to your life. Proverbs 9:9-11 (NIV)

In late 1969, Bishop Muzorewa appointed Alec to be Interim Education Secretary for the Rhodesia Annual Conference with an office at Church Headquarters in Salisbury. We moved December 10 on a flatbed truck to a rental home on Montague Avenue. The house was just vacated by the Education Secretary, who was going on furlough. This was a big move because we moved from a large African community to a large European (white) community. The communities were vastly different in a country under the rule of apartheid (separation of peoples). The school year was divided into three terms. This move took place after the close of the last term in 1969 and the beginning of the first term in 1970. As Interim Education Secretary, Alec was responsible for all the schools in the country under the Methodist Church.

On January 9, 1970, we received a telegram from my mother telling us that my brother Lindsey had a fire at his house. His nine-month-old daughter was lost in the fire. This was my niece that I had never met and would never meet here on Earth. My mother and I could only share sorrow long distance. My mother would call and just hold the telephone to hear my voice, she was so moved she could not speak, only cry. She would pay for the calls to hear only. The

85

excruciating pain prevented her ability to speak. It was so hard to be so far away. We had stored things at Lindsey's house and those items were lost. While we were sad that all our family photos were gone, our loss was nothing compared to what Lindsey and his wife had lost.

We remained in this appointment from December 1969 until April 1970, when George Fleshman, the full time Education Secretary, returned from furlough. Veranita celebrated her first birthday during this time and the children enjoyed dog sitting for the Fleshman's dog. Lex celebrated his eighth birthday with a party. Karen was pleased to have ballet lessons at Blakiston School where she and Lex were students. The school was close enough for them to walk. They needed uniforms for school, and we were fortunate that the school maintained a school closet so we could buy used uniforms very reasonably. In April we returned all the school uniforms and moved again. We were very proficient in packing and moving.

Chapter Fourteen: Another Move

For in Him we live and move and have our being. As some of your own poets have said, "We are His offspring." Acts 17:28 (NIV)

The United Methodist Church owned a 14-room house, known as the hostel, used for the children of missionaries serving in places too far from schools. These white missionary children were not allowed to attend the African schools, just like we were not able to have Karen and Lex in the African schools at the other mission sites we served. The house was located near Epworth Theological College. The children would remain at the hostel Monday through Friday, allowing them to attend school. Their parents would collect them on Fridays and return them on Sunday.

There was an interesting formation of rocks nearby on Epworth Mission, a British Methodist Mission Station. Very large rocks balanced on a very small rock. These Balancing Rocks always made us think of the present situation in Rhodesia. The government was attempting a balancing act to maintain the privileged position of the white 5% of the population against the just aspirations of the black 95%. Could they do it? NO! Policies based on privilege and self-interest were ultimately doomed. Black nationalists were equipping and preparing for an intensifying civil war. The white government continued to hold on to the reins of power.

We were appointed as Hostel Parents. The Hostel had a VW bus for transporting the children to the doctor, music, sports, swimming, and church. We had children from other Protestant faiths being cared for at the hostel. There were some children that were at the hostel consistently and then there were other children that came for short term stays. Sometimes their parents were in hospital or traveling for special projects. So, we never knew how many children would be in the house at any given time.

It was very sad that one of our hostel children, just six years old, lost his mother during our term there. His family was working as missionaries under the British Methodist Church. Peter often would wet the bed in the night; take off his clothes and crawl in the bed with us. Peter's father wrote a beautiful statement of the lost wife and mother and shared it with us. It is found in Appendix C of this book. As I read it for the first time, I realized that this writing reflected a lot of what I felt for God and for Africa.

The Hostel was quite modern for the time. We had a black and white television with one channel. There were only broadcasts of shows in the evening from 5pm to 10pm. Mostly the shows were in English. Superman or Lassie was extremely popular. Most of the shows were from the United States. However, we also had the BBC for news. The children did not spend much time watching the television because they had schoolwork to do, or they played outside when they had free time. The children also had chores to do. The house had 14 rooms and while we had staff to help, the children still had to help keep their rooms clean.

While at the hostel, Alec also taught Old Testament studies at Epworth Theological College. I helped the women at Highfield Church through sewing classes. I was also working with the United Methodist Women as Dean of the Leadership School. Alec cared for the children to enable me to go for the Leadership Training School. Karen was old enough to share in the care of Veranita. I had to wean Veranita before I left.

After our leadership training session, we took a bus trip with 138 women and four babies to Zimbabwe Ruins. Zimbabwe Ruins is the site of a city known as Great Zimbabwe which used to be a large and wealthy trading area. Archeologists have found signs of ancient items from Persia and China. The trip was a one-week event that was the culmination of the leadership event. There were three buses loaded with women, all wearing the RRW Uniform. It was a wonderful sight. But since we were a mixed group, we could not stop along the way for a rest stop at a public service station, so we stopped along the side of the road for a comfort break and go in the woods. I parked my car behind the hostel's VW bus. When finished, we were getting back in the vehicles when the bus backed over the top of my car crushing the window screen. Thank goodness no one was in the car. While at Zimbabwe Ruins, women bowed and kneeled in gratitude to God for all that He had done for them.

My informant from Language School, Shebbaoh Chidzekwe, had written that she was in the hospital in Umtali and since we would be coming that way, she asked me to come visit her. When she wrote me to come, I did not realize she had cholera and was in the isolation hospital. There was a huge sign outside the hospital that read, "Enter Here at Your own RISK" Infectious Disease Hospital. I entered for a quick visit and a prayer on my lips. I visited and as I was leaving her, she shouted to me, "ALL WOULD BE LOST WITHOUT JESUS CHRIST." This was said to the truth about Rhodesia. Rhodesia would be lost without Jesus Christ. There is only one hope for this land, Jesus Christ. Without the Love of God and Christian concern for ALL, there is no hope. God was good and Shebbaoh Chidzekwe was treated and did get well.

We had remained at the hostel until May 1971, when the Leadership Training School was over. We rode the train to South Africa to board the boat for our second furlough. I was so tired I slept the whole three days we were on the train. We went to Cape Town to board the passenger ship, Windsor Castle, for a trip up the west coast of Africa.

We were on the Windsor Castle for a month. The five of us had a suite with a side room that had bunk beds. It was exciting when we crossed the equator. The ship staff arranged for a crossing celebration which was great fun for the children and us. A pole was put across the pool, and it was lubricated, making it very slippery. Two adults would then get to the middle of the pole and compete to see who would win. Because the competition was fierce, children were not allowed to compete. The adults would hit each other with pillowcases filled with balloons. The winner was the one who stayed on the slippery pole without being knocked into the pool below. It was sort of like an ocean cruise version of the King of the Mountain game. Alec gave it a try but did not survive his round. He was knocked off and fell to the pool.

During the equator crossing celebration, the cruise crew dressed up as Neptune with a trident or mermaids. The pool was dyed green with shark propellant and one of the crew dove in. In another place a crew member had another staff person in a barber chair and was pretending to do surgery. There was fake blood all over the place and the pretend surgeon pulled a sausage out of the victim's abdomen, pretending to be removing intestines. It was all done in fun. Each evening we dressed for dinner and on some days, we had ports of call where we could leave the ship for day trips and excursions. It was a luxurious time after working so hard in Rhodesia with little time off for vacation.

When we arrived in England, before going on to the United States, we left the ship planning to visit some friends. We rented a car but then discovered it was a holiday in England and there was not enough time to do all that we had planned because businesses were closed and our friends unavailable. We did have enough time to purchase a brand-new Volvo station wagon at a very good price. We were going to need a reliable car when we got to New York. So, we purchased it and had it loaded on the ship. We were on the last leg of our trip home.

Part V: Second Furlough

Come to me, all of you who are tired from carrying heavy loads,

and I will give you rest.

Matthew 11:28 (GNTD)

Chapter Fifteen: Study Leave

But if you look closely into the perfect law that sets people free and keep on paying attention to it and do not simply listen and then forget it but put it into practice- you will be blessed by God in what you do. James 1:25 (GNTD)

The ship landed in New York, and we visited the General Board of Global Ministries for debriefing on May 31st. We took delivery of the Volvo Station Wagon in New Jersey. Unfortunately, the car had been vandalized and the radio was taken. We aren't sure if this happened on the ship or in the shipyards.

This furlough was like our first furlough; we needed to watch and pray! When the business with the mission board was complete, we drove south to visit my parents in Birmingham, Alabama. On the way we stopped to visit church friends in Big Pond-Wetona, Pennsylvania, where we served 1958-59 just before we left for Rhodesia our first term. We also visited Pinnacle, North Carolina, where we served in 1965-67. It was wonderful to see so many friends

We had been working part time at Epworth Theological College in Rhodesia and it left us thinking that with more theological education we would be better teachers. Alec was teaching Old Testament and I was working in the school for the wives during that time.

June was a busy furlough month for us. While in Birmingham, we visited the North Alabama Annual Conference when it was in session. While there they took the vote on the merger of the North

Alabama Conference with the Central Jurisdiction Conference in Alabama. It passed by one vote. This merger was taking a primarily white conference and a primarily black conference and creating one conference in the United Methodist Church. The narrow win only magnified how sharply divided race relations were in the United States.

While on furlough, we were on the road a lot and the children went with us. My mother and father were aging, and the kids were growing. It made it difficult for our children to stay with my parents because my parents just did not know the kids' routines of care. I did not want to burden my parents. From Alabama we went to Lake Junaluska and attended the Western North Carolina Annual Conference. While there we saw Dr. J.C. Peters, a Black District Superintendent, elected on the first ballot to lead the ministerial delegation from the Annual Conference to General Conference. Encouraging changes have taken place during the four years we have been away. We then went to the missionary conference held at Scarritt College in Nashville. This was a time of self-examination and also inspiration. During the conference, we saw several films about the problems that confronted us in the world at that time. Two problems stood out, one about South Africa and the other about Argentina. We realized more clearly than ever about the oppression that existed in the world.

We were thankful for the opportunity to visit one of our supporting churches at Langdale, Alabama. It was wonderful to meet members of the church as we had been to Langdale previously. We count it a great privilege to be one of the groups of missionaries who have been supported by this mission-minded church through the years.

We were able to visit Dot's home church in Birmingham, Central Park United Methodist, as a family in July before Alec left for Harvard to do language study. During July and August, with Alec away, I visited many churches and groups in Alabama to share with them the concerns of the church in Rhodesia. I also spent a week at Sumatanga Camp and Conference Center in Alabama attending the North Alabama Conference Schools of Missions for the Women's Society of Christian Service (WSCS) and Wesleyan Service Guild (WSG). Both of these groups were predecessors of the United Methodist Women.

When Alec finished his studies and returned in August, we visited our other supporting church at Conover, North Carolina. It was a joy to be there again, and it brought back memories of our first visit to Conover just before we returned to Rhodesia in 1967.

In late August we went to Durham as Alec had been accepted at Duke as a special student to do language study before he could become a doctoral candidate. Lex started school at Fernbank for 5th grade and Karen was at Druid Hills for 7th grade. Mom Alvord, Nancy and Elizabeth, Alec's sisters, came to our home at Holly Hills Apartments for a weeklong visit during their time in the United States. We took them to sites in Durham that none of us had been to before. We also drove to Pinnacle so that Nancy and Elizabeth could see Pilot Mountain.

The apartment complex was rather large. We were able to associate with the other families in the complex and a lot of them had children the same age as ours. Karen and Lex had a lot of playmates. Lex had a Big Wheel, a riding device similar to a tricycle but closer to the ground. He drove it all over the complex. We were in a two-bedroom apartment. We had cable television for the first time, and we enjoyed television with no commercials! I did not work as we only had one car and Alec had to use it to get to the Divinity School on the other side of campus. Plus, I took care of the children. Karen was twelve at the time and one of our neighbors was a neonatologist at Duke Hospital. Karen became interested in the medical field. She often would babysit for the doctor. He found out about her interest and would take her to the hospital with him occasionally to make rounds on his patients. He even let her wear a white lab coat.

The situation in Rhodesia was such that the editor of our church magazine was summoned to appear in the Umtali Regional Court to face five charges under the Law and Order (Maintenance) Act for items printed in our church magazine. Bishop Muzorewa was taken off a train traveling to Mozambique. He was banned by the Rhodesian Government from entering the Tribal Trust Lands in Rhodesia where most of the Methodist churches were situated.

When school started in September 1972 we were at a new school and on to a new experience as Alec began studies in Old Testament at Emory University in Atlanta, Georgia. We looked forward to an enriching experience as we continued to prepare ourselves for further service in Rhodesia. Karen and Lex are making good adjustments to their new schools. Veranita found many friends here at the Clifton Court Apartments   It was in married student housing just across the street from the Centers for Communicable Disease (CDC). We started in a one-bedroom apartment but then had the opportunity to move to a two bedroom as soon as one became available. Our family had a wonderful church relationship with Trinity Church in downtown Atlanta. I had the same situation in that I did not work. Alec had to use the car to get to Candler School of Theology and I had to care for the children.

Since coming to Atlanta, we had much concern for Rhodesia and for Bishop Muzorewa. He had spoken in Atlanta and was known to many. Rhodesia was in the news that summer. The entire Rhodesian team, of black and white athletes, were originally banned from attending the Olympics because of the political strife in Rhodesia. The European White government in Rhodesia had cut the final link with the United Kingdom by declaring Rhodesia a republic. The International Olympic Committee (IOC) said that the Rhodesian team could participate only if they competed under the old flag, which they agreed to do. After arriving in Munich for the Olympic Games, the teams from other African countries objected to the presence of the Rhodesian team because of the segregation in Rhodesia. The pressure from the African teams was so intense, the IOC then changed the team's status, and the team was not permitted to participate in the games. The reaction in Rhodesia was strong. There was discrimination and denial of basic human rights to the black community. So, the other African teams were correct in their objections. Will the Rhodesian white government look deeply at themselves and ask, "Why did this happen? Why are they not accepted by the rest of the world?" What can we do to correct our relationships with other peoples?" Unfortunately, the white government did not do that introspection and the tension grew between the peoples of Rhodesia.

Black guerrilla forces attacked the northern part of Rhodesia and wanted to overthrow the white government. Then when they found they couldn't do that, they attacked government workers, vandalized government property, raided and killed white farmers who had a reputation for being severe masters. The white government, in retaliation, initiated a very brutal counterattack. And the people of Rhodesia were caught in the middle. African leadership continued to emerge from the African community. In December Bishop Muzorewa accepted chairmanship of the African National Council, a new organization formed to represent the unified majority against the Anglo-Rhodesian Settlement Proposals. These proposals were intended to settle long-standing differences between the British government and the Smith regime. The proposals, however, were negotiated without consultation with Africans and did not satisfy the African desire for self-rule. In March 1972, The A.N.C. declared itself a political party under leadership of Bishop Muzorewa, its President. Bishop Muzorewa was not a political person. He was the shepherd of the church.

What can solve the problems of this land? Only the blood of Christ. The only hope of the world can be found in each person opening their heart to the LOVE of God. Then, and only then, can the promise of Micah become a reality.

The word of the LORD shall go forth. He shall judge between many peoples. And they shall beat their swords into plowshares, and their spears into pruning hooks. Nation shall not lift up sword against nation, neither shall they learn war anymore. and none shall make them afraid; for the mouth of the LORD of hosts has spoken. We will walk in the name of the LORD our God forever and ever.
Micah 4:2b-5

Our period of study came to an end when we received a letter from Bishop Muzorewa telling us that Alec had been appointed as Education Secretary for the Rhodesia Annual Conference. He was to replace George Fleshman who would be going to Maun in Botswana. This work would not be completely new to Alec as he served as acting Education Secretary for a few months in 1970 while George Fleshman was on furlough.

The main thrust of Alec's work would be with the Headmasters and Principals of our five major institutions, Murewa, Mutambara, Nyadiri, Nyamuzwe and Old Umtali. We have high schools at each of these centers and our major educational work was done through these schools. In addition, Nyadiri had a teachers' training college where we trained teachers for primary schools. These institutions were vital as the young people who attended these schools were the leaders of the future.

We looked forward to our return. I would be involved in women's work again, helping with 200 home craft clubs and participating in the life of the church. The home craft clubs were similar to home economics classes in the United States. High school aged girls would come from all over the region to the center located at the Language School in Nyaksapa. The home craft schools were a substitute for school. The girls did not have funds to attend regular school. They did not have a seat at the local school. Also, without money, the girls could not stay in the dorms. Sometimes a girl's family would provide dorm or classes cost by donating a cow. If the girls could not stay in the dorm, they would live with neighbors nearby. They would stay at the center for one year.

Some of the girls in the Home Craft School.

At the center, the girls learned how to cook and sew. There were local artisans who taught special crafts, such as making grass mats. The girls would learn to use sewing machines. A friend of ours in the United States Navy sent several sewing machines to the center. While at the center, the girls would get a certificate that would then help them get jobs. They would leave the center and become nannies or maids. My primary job at the center would be to hire staff to teach the children. Sometimes, I had to remove a teacher. I was looking forward to returning to Rhodesia to pick up this work.

We left Atlanta in early December 1973. We found a buyer for our Volvo who agreed to let us use the car until we arrived at the airport. We boarded South African Airways to return to Rhodesia for a third time.

Part VI: Third Term of Service

Whatever you do, work at it with all your heart, as though you were working for the Lord and not for people.

Colossians 3:23 (GNTD)

Chapter Sixteen: Education Secretary

Each one, as a good manager of God's different gifts, must use for the good of others the special gift he has received from God. 1 Peter 4:10 (GNTD)

Bishop Muzorewa had given Alec the date of December 9th for the time he should be in Rhodesia. This would mean he would not be able to complete the exams for his PhD. We left Emory having completed all the course work but no exams. We returned to the Hostel which is where we were when we left in 1971. Lex went back to primary school as if he had never left. Karen was enrolled at Waterford in Swaziland. This was a boarding school that was paid for by the Board of Mission. The Board paid for the tuition and travel to and from the school. We were leaving her 900 miles from home in a boarding school in an independent African country for what we thought would be a good environment. We left her there on the way back to Rhodesia. One of the hardest chapters in my life. Karen was 14 years old at the time and Alec and I had heard about this school from other missionary families. Because of that, she was in the company of other missionary kids, including some families from Rhodesia. It was a medium sized secondary school. She only came home at quarter break. She and the other children from Rhodesia flew together and it was a direct flight from Swaziland to Salisbury. While there Karen thrived.

Back in Rhodesia, the civil war was escalating. We came back to more guerrilla warfare and the Rhodesian government began to conscript white males aged 38 to 50. Luckily, or maybe God blessed, Alec was not drafted because he had the responsibility of traveling to other countries in Africa, representing the Rhodesian Annual Conference of the United Methodist Church. Bishop Muzorewa could not travel because he was leading one of the major political factions. We often had to help Bishop Muzorewa hide because of the death threats he received. Once Alec had to hide Bishop Muzorewa in our car and drive him out of Salisbury. It was a very dangerous time to be in Rhodesia, but we knew that God had led us back for this time of service and He would see us equipped to do our work.

One such blessing was seen at the Hostel. There were a lot of cutbacks for the school from the government and the Annual Conference. We were blessed by having children come from different African countries. Some came from countries not embroiled in civil war, and from different faith denominations. This got us through the times when we had to make sure our 18 children at the Hostel had what they needed. God's promise for a purpose was played out even when the bayonets flashed in history.

The decrease in church support for World Service and Global Ministries in America hurt us and caused the curtailment of many programs. The total budget for education was cut from $11,000 to $600 in one year! Our Christian Education program was cut completely, and our Conference Extension work cut to the barest minimum. Our Conference Evangelism program was cut in half. This placed a heavy burden on our local pastors as they strived to meet the growing needs of an increasing membership in the church. In the midst of conflict of war, the people of Rhodesia found comfort in God's words and God's promises of deliverance.

In Alec's role of Education Secretary for the Annual Conference, we found critical shortage of places for our African youth to continue their education. As demand for dwindling upper-level classes grew, acceptance in Form VI (Junior College) was 3.7 on a 4-point grading scale. Due to the war, there just weren't enough teachers and administrators to meet the demand. We had the same kind of situation for those children completing grade school and the cry was for more schools. We could not even expand our present schools because the Board of Ministries had no funds for buildings. Giving in our United States churches had fallen behind.

At a meeting of the headmasters of our six post primary schools, this fact was driven home. The Rhodesian Government Ministry of Education wanted to expand high school education in Rhodesia and gave us permission to add additional classes. The caveat was that we had to provide staff houses and classrooms. Local resources were very limited. The Board of Global Ministries had no funds. Thus, children had no place for school. The dream of a better, more equitable Rhodesia for all people, would not and could not be lived out.

Over the following years, civil war continued and life in Rhodesia deteriorated. Deaths from fighting increased and the possibility of peacefully transferring power from the minority to the majority disappeared. Over the last four years, any person, white or black, that could get out of the country did so. With that, the minority of the whites dwindled even more. The Rhodesian government began to recruit whites from other countries, trying to maintain the power. While we tried to carry on with mission work, God's work, it became increasingly evident that we were going to have to leave.

In 1977, the decision was made. We were reading the newspaper article that the Rhodesian government would begin to draft white

Rhodesians in greater numbers. The age of white males was lowered to fifteen and the length of service went from one year to 18 months. It was a knife to our hearts, but we knew we had to make plans. This new draft would take both Alec and Lex. It was so hard to accept the change. Change went against our call. Our call was from God and this war was brought on by men's voices seeking war. There were people, some we knew and many that we did not, who could not get out of danger's path and that made us sad. We had given close to 20 years of service to Rhodesia. We knew in our hearts that the changes would come, and our prayers would be with them every step of the way. Even if our physical presence wasn't there.

By the time we made our decision, the other 100 missionaries in the country had already left. It was a scary time and the local Africans that were in mission with us knew we had to go. Alec's family had all already emigrated to other countries. We had United States passports so we knew where we would go. Still, it took us several weeks to make all the arrangements. There were so many personal items we had to leave behind. Lex was at boarding school several hours away and we had to get him. Karen was in boarding school still in Swaziland and we would collect her on the way to the ship in South Africa. We finally made it to the train that would take us to South Africa. While going through ticketing, officials were checking for any white male who should be serving in the army. They were making sure no one was leaving illegally. They looked hard at Alec and Lex's paperwork and threatened to not let us get on the train. Once they confirmed that the United States passports were legitimate, we were able to board the train to leave. We were on the train for three days, including the stop to pick up Karen. We finally boarded the ship in Cape Town and began our last journey away from our beloved Africa. The 13,000-mile trip by ship to New York would last many weeks.

When we finally arrived and had our debrief with the General Board of Global Missions, we knew our days of mission in Rhodesia were over. We still have hope for the African people to finally achieve majority rule. We prayed for war to end and God's will to be done. Shortly after we left, Prime Minister Ian Smith conceded the government to Bishop Muzorewa. Prayers from all over the world were answered. It would take several more years for the majority government to stabilize. The country would be named Zimbabwe.

We arrived in the United States in April, and we had several months before Alec would be assigned to a church in the Western North Carolina Conference. We were going back to the area where he had served during his study time at Duke. During those months we stayed with my mother and father for a few weeks. My brother, Lindsey, helped us get a car. It was a special treat because the car was in immaculate condition, especially the engine that was built by the mechanic for NASCAR legend Bobby Allison. The car was a super star. We drove all over the United States, seeing national treasures and visiting areas with links to our family. Mostly we slept in a tent but occasionally we stayed in a motel. Soon, it was time to begin mission in a different way. We were assigned to a two-church charge, Advance United Methodist Church, and Mocks United Methodist Church, in Advance, North Carolina. While we had left Rhodesia, God still called us to be about His work in new and exciting ways. All we had to do was let Him lead.

Appendix A: The Legend of the Black Madonna

The Legend of the Black Madonna.

Doris Lessing, 1966

Once upon a time a magnificent church was being built in a certain city and there was need for one great stained-glass window to go in a certain conspicuous wall. The committees in charge felt that it would be wise to have artists from all over the world submit designs for this window. Many very famous painters entered drawings in the contest, finally the one design on which all the committee agreed unanimously was made by an artist of unknown name and fame. They commissioned him forthwith to go ahead with the work and to have all in readiness for the dedication of the church on Christmas Eve.

The unknown artist saw in it a chance to work out a certain grudge which he had against all mankind—a grudge so deep and bitter that he thought of it day and night and kept himself secluded in his attic studio rather than try to mix with people whom he hated. So, he took the sketch which the committee approved so enthusiastically and made certain little changes here and there with almost wicked delight and then he called his wife and baby so they could pose for the enlarged painting which he must make.

Now it happened hat his wife had been hanging the family washing and she came wearing a shawl over her head and carrying the baby in the clothes basket. After she put down the basket she leaned over it, then looking up, said gently, "Sh! The baby is sound asleep. If I pick him up, he will wake and cry."

"Don't pick him up," cried the artist, "Stay just as you are; that pose is perfect. Imagine that the clothes basket is a manger, that you are Mary, the mother of Jesus, and you have leaned over to see if He is sleeping, but now you look up because you hear the approach of someone—someone outside on camels the three Wise Men. Here at the top of the canvas, see I shall paint the star that came and stood over the place where the young child lay. Stay perfectly still, dear…fine."

So, the painter's wife kept the pose that he thought was so perfect and with perfect, sure strokes he painted her as she knelt there. And it was a far lovelier picture than he had planned to make it, because in the heart of his wife there was none of the bitter grudge that was in his heart. For when she looked down at her sleeping child a great peace stole over her.

Day after day the posing continued, until finally the artist had finished the picture, it was ready for the stained-glass workers. And here his difficulty lay, for if they discovered his secret everything would be spoiled. He thought of a plan—a clever, secret plan that could not help but work out as he wished. The week before Christmas the various parts of the window arrived in that distant city where the Church of the Redeemer was already completed. Trained workers began assembling the bits of glass and putting them in place, when a strange oversight bewildered them, neither face nor arms of the Madonna and child could be found. The workmen were nearly frantic until the artist arrived and calmed their fears by saying that he had brought the missing parts of the window with him and he, himself, would put them in place later. It was a whim of his to put the face and arms in himself, after the rest of the window was ready. When they discovered that he had mastered the correct process of fastening the extra pieces of glass in place, it was only natural that they agreed to his request.

When the time arrived for the dedication of the church on Christmas Eve, the artist slipped inconspicuously into the back pew, for he was unknown as yet to the committee. And just as he had imagined, the dedication service proceeded as had been planned, but when the last carol had been sung and the benediction had been pronounced, it was very noticeable that groups of people clustered in the aisles, and everybody was looking toward the window.

"The face of that Madonna is certainly black," they were saying. "She looks exactly like a black person. Even the baby looks like a black baby. Where is that artist, anyhow? The original sketch was not like this. Certainly, the glass factory would never have let such an error pass their inspector. Somebody has done us an injury. We cannot permit such a window in this magnificent church."

The artist, lurking behind a pillar, chuckled with glee. "Paying back, all you white Christians, all you superior, disagreeable, lordly beings. Paying back for all the years of insult you heaped on a poor black artist." And his face grew hard with hatred and spite.

Now is the time to tell you of the minister. He was a good man and a gentle man. He had lain awake all-night wondering, wondering how he was going to preach the sermon he had announced from the text which was printed in that now famous window. "In Him was Life and the Life was the Light of men." John 1:4. He had intended to build his sermon around the window; and tell how the hopes of all mankind clustered about the place where the young Child lay. But now, should he point to the window, to the Black Madonna and Child? He could hardly eat any breakfast and walked into the chancel with a miserable sinking in his heart."

"I must preach about the window just as I had planned," he said to himself. "But Oh Lord, help me to find words to say." Yet he really had not the least idea of what he would say, even when he rose and announced his text: "In Him is Life, and the Life was the Light of men."

The congregation was reading these very words in the glass of the window, and some were resenting such words under such a picture, when suddenly the winter sun came blazing forth that Christmas morning with all the extra dazzle of a snowy day, and its brightness came beaming through the stained-glass window. A gasp of sheer surprise spread through the church; for in that blaze of sunlight the Madonna's face was shining, pure as an angel's face, and the little Child's face was a sheen of dazzling glory. Inspired by the miracle of the transfigured Black Madonna and Child, the minister preached a sermon that marked a milestone in the life of every person present.

"Who are you and I to say we do not want a Black Madonna in our church? In that great day of beginnings when the Lord God made man, did he signify, 'Let us make white man in our image. Let us make man'? And to some He gave dark skin, to some white; He must have seen little difference in these external colors, for there are four hundred million yellow in Asia and India with three hundred million brown and America with several hundred million white men. So, in deep humility this Christmas Day I ask you—Last night when the Savior looked down into this church of the Redeemer, who looked really black to His all-seeing gaze? —that Black Madonna or you and me? With black consternation in our hearts, because we felt, of course, a Madonna needed flesh the shade of our flesh."

"Oh, the conceits of us, the curious blackness in our hearts that cannot see God shine through flesh of another color; but now that we have seen this miracle demonstrated, we need only to turn our eyes to the wonderful face of that black mother—was there ever tenderness like hers. Like Mary of old she seems to keep all these things and ponder them in her heart. Have you forgotten the old familiar Bible story of how when God sent His own little Son to earth, He did not choose a white-skinned mother for Him, but one whose cheeks were olive tan—a Jew, let us then this Christmas Morning be Wise-men, bringing our gifts to the Savior of all mankind; and the place where the young child lay, let us put the most difficult thing to give up—our race prejudice!"

There was a curious sequel to his sermon. Although you may be expecting to hear first what the congregation did, the artist himself did something unexpected, and it left everyone breathless. With faltering steps, he walked to the pulpit and placed in the minister's hand a package, explaining brokenly, "It is my Christmas present to the Church which I have wronged so insanely and selfishly. So here are the original pieces of glass for the faces and arms of the Madonna and Child. I substituted the black myself. I wanted to prove to you what hypocrites you Christians were, that there was nothing to your religion, but snobbish superiority. But you have shown me that I was wrong, that in the sight of God Almighty there is neither black nor white, when His light shines through. Tomorrow, I shall change the Black Madonna, today I give my gift—I give up my hate to the Savior. I am ashamed—I learned my lesson when the glory of His light shone through."

Then the congregation said, "We too have learned a lesson. Let us leave the Black Madonna in its place forever, so that our children and children's children may see how the light that comes to earth with the Christ-child is indeed the Light of the world, shining through the faces of God's family, whatever color the faces may be."

Appendix B: Shared Letters with other Missionaries

<u>Another story of Arnoldine from our missionary friends living there.</u>

After we had finished six months of Shona language training at Nyakatsapa, Norm was appointed conference director of Christian education. We stayed there at Nyakatsapa for another six months, and I continued to work with Mai Chiunda on language. Meanwhile, as Norm traveled about from district to district, he was keeping his eye open for a likely place to live, as we had decided that his appointment gave us freedom to live outside the confines of a "mission station". At one time he was seriously considering Muziti, but the local folks there were uncertain about such a venture, and the folks at Arnoldine more open to the possibility. So, we moved there after Christmas, 1962, in hopes of getting Paul started in first grade in January. Bruce, our third child, was an infant of six weeks when we moved there, so it would have been mid-January. The district superintendent at that time, Rev. Luke Chieza had already pre-selected Mai Rukunda as the person to work for our family, taking care of children, cooking, etc. Mai (mother) was selected for several reasons, I believe, such as the fact that she was a natural leader, calm in manner, about my age, and HER mother, Mbuya (grandmother) Mbwizhu, was such a leader in the church. And so, we began building our life there. Paul seemed to enjoy going to school, although it took three months for us figure out that he was not learning to read. So, the first-grade teacher volunteered to work with him extra hours beyond school hours, and he improved.

I believe it was after we had been there for about five months, but am uncertain about dates, that I became "strangely" ill - and Norm left on his appointed rounds, thinking that I just had a "bug" and would soon be better. But things got worse, and someone from the village managed to drive me to Rusape Hospital, where I blurted out that I was "Peeing coca cola" and felt terrible. I was admitted immediately.

Apparently great effort was made to tract down Norm, and a message sent for him to come home, as I had left the four children in the care of Mai Rukunda, and as I said, this was all fairly new for her and for us. Norm came home, visited me, then went home to the children. The next day I lay in my bed and heard his footsteps coming down the hall. The nurse said, "Hello, Mr. Thomas, are you here to see your wife?" "No!" he blurted, "I'm sick too!" So, he was admitted in the next room. At some point shortly after that, you came to the hospital and told me that you had been to Arnoldine and taken the children, together with Mai Rukunda to help you, to care for them all. Was that really how it happened? Or did Norm take them to you? I do not think so. I really was quite ill at that point, and little memory of anything except the deep gratitude I felt for your readiness to do such a thing. I do remember feeling grateful for spirit in which it was all done. Not condemning, not critical even, although Mai had not known how to prevent Bruce from developing a whopping diaper rash. She did not realize how much more tender little white bottoms could be. How long did you have the family? I do not know, but it was surely a matter of a few weeks, at least? It amazes me that we were not closer friends after that, but I am sure our lives just went in different ways, and I felt burdened with such a feeling of indebtedness to you.

Everyone at Arnoldine seemed to think that we had been bewitched because we were living in the abandoned homestead of an African family in which the wife was barren and they had sought help from Mai Chaza, who was known for the angels who would come in the night and get barren women pregnant.

At any rate, the villagers were sure we would flee those haunted environs, but we lived there, quite happily, I might add, for three years. It was the Rhodesian government that did us in by denying the chance for the children to continue in the local school.

Story shared by our friend Winnie Thomas used by permission.

The year is 1961 and it marks a new beginning for Southern Rhodesia now a "Land of Decision", and there are many decisions to be made. Make no mistake, the drumbeats of freedom cannot and will not be silenced. They echo and re-echo around the world; and so, they should. The cry for freedom is not harsh on the ears of the missionaries. We only hope that the church can take an active part in teaching what freedom is. Kwacha! Freedom! But freedom doesn't mean a big parade; it means more responsibility. Freedom doesn't mean everyone can own a car without working; it means being able to keep what you work hard enough to get. Freedom doesn't mean that everyone must respect you; it means you must respect the freedom of everyone else. This is what we must teach, so that when Kwacha comes, she will be recognized and welcomed, not as something that is easy, but as something that is necessary for the human dignity of man.

Excerpts taken from a letter of Marjorie Smock,
short-term missionary,

1960 sent to supporting churches used by permission

This year as you think about Southern Rhodesia, please remember that her people are REAL. They have personalities, they have individual wants and desires, they have strengths and weaknesses in their character, and they have bodies, minds, and souls. Think of them as people just as real and just as individualistic as yourselves. May your prayer for them be that they might realize their hopes and dreams for equality, for a government that practices a policy of "Partnership," and for an eagle-like Africa that will fly on until it reaches the upper sky where the air is pure and free!

God Bless Africa.

Appendix C: A Tribute to Margaret

God has a plan for each of us

And will fulfill His purposes and His plan if we give our lives into His hands.

At such time as this it is possible to look back

And recognize the pattern and plan of God,

There was a special moment on a special day,

> Eleven o'clock in the evening, May 2nd, 1960,

> when we held hands and knew that we had 'come home' to each other.

That day marked our engagement.

We could not know then how significant the time and date would be.

In her early days Margaret trusted Christ as her Savior and Lord

> Giving her life into His hands.

She allowed Him to work out His perfect plan.

> She drew strength and guidance from constant reading of His word,

> And received direction for her life as she communed with God in prayer.

Her love for God and her many gifts

Found fulfillment in her zeal to win others for Christ-

Girls at South End High School, at University,

And in later years, at Roosevelt High School in Salisbury.

As Margaret matured, her zeal increased.

And her love for others widened to include those of other lands,

While still a schoolgirl

She took the opportunity to meet folk from India and Africa,

And went all out to befriend them.

It was laid upon her heart to serve African women in Rhodesia,

To visit them in their homes, to help them care for their families,

To tell them of her Lord and teach them His word,

She taught European children in Salisbury,

And helped the African Sunday School in Vavambi and Harare.

Our marriage opened the way by which she could more fully respond to this call,

Kwenda, Old Umtali Biblical Institute, Epworth Theological College

Each gave her opportunity to serve and teach.

Margaret – Mother.

God gave us children.

She was there to nurse, care, teach and watch over each one:

Peter, Graham,-Linda, and Alison - a complete family.

But the call was strong

> To reach the African people in the more remote areas of Rhodesia:

> To serve Gokwe.

To respond to God's call to go there –

> And for the family to remain united together –

> Meant that, for two years, Margaret taught the three eldest by herself.

It was hard,

> But for love of God and love of her children she did it gladly and well.

It was great fun to be with her, in the schoolroom, in the garden,

> searching for adventure on a walk through the 'bundu,'

> > as we called the African bush,

> > or on a hot dusty day

> > Enjoying the cool water in the swimming bath at Gokwe.

She was our Mother,

On May 3rd this week, I was with the children.

Linda started singing: -

"Jesus loves me, this I know,

For the Bible tells me so."

"Yes," I said, "but it is important to <u>know</u> in your heart that this <u>is</u> true.

God has so wonderfully guided and helped us.

He delivered both Mummy and Daddy from death in 1958.

Mummy was very sick,

Daddy had a car accident,

But He rescued us both and gave us to one another

He gave you to us to love,

And as He had a plan for Mummy and Daddy, so He has a plan for you.

He has led us in the past through many moves and changes

And has especially helped us while Mummy has been so ill.

You know how much pain she has suffered.

When Mummy prayed to God she said: -

'Please, Lord, either give me full health and strength

so that I can look after my family,

Or take me home to be with you.'

God knew that He could not give her the first request

So, He gave her the second.

The pain left her, but she was so weak.

Then came our Special Day-

      The anniversary of the day on which, eleven years before,

      We told each other of our love.

The time was eleven pm when God called – 'Come Home" –

And Mummy heard Him and went.

So, we thought about Mummy, and cried a little.

Later, when they were in bed, we were talking together.

"But we've still got the films and photos," said Peter.

"Those are only pictures," I answered.

"They will remind us of happy memories, but that's all."

"Listen," I said. "I love Mummy. Not "I loved Mummy."

Mummy loves you. Not Mummy loved you.'

We cannot go to her and we cannot see her, but we know

      That Mummy is with Jesus, and Jesus is with us."

      That Mummy is near us –and all is well

"And God our Father is with us too," said Graham,

"So, Mummy is near us – and all is well," I ended.

And this is what she is saying to you, right now.

'Turn over and go to sleep.'"

And without another word, they did.

About the Author

Born in 1937, in Town Creek, Alabama, Dot grew up in a southern lifestyle. An active member of her community, she could be found on the stage in school plays, on the football field playing the clarinet, or twirling on the skating rink.

Accepted as a short-term missionary by the Women's Division of the General Board of Global Ministries of the United Methodist Church in 1958, Dot met her husband, Alec Alvord, at the training program for new missionaries held at Scarritt College in Nashville, Tennessee. Accepted as career missionaries, they were commissioned for service and arrived in Zimbabwe, then known as Rhodesia, in May 1959.

During three terms of service between 1959 and 1977, Dot served as president of a local United Methodist Women (UMW) unit, taught Bible classes in school, participated in women's Home Craft clubs and was Co-Dean of the Zimbabwe Annual Conference Leadership Training School for the Rukwadzano (UMW) for two years. Dot also served as Director of the Nyakatsapa Home Craft School for girls unable to find a place in regular high schools.

Since completing her missionary service in Zimbabwe in 1977, Dot taught in multiple public-school systems in North Carolina, United States. She retired to care for her father in her home until his death.

She has served as Vice President and President of the Western North Carolina Annual Conference Clergy Partners. She has been active in the UMW in Western North Carolina where she has served as District Coordinator of Christian Global Concerns in the North Wilkesboro District and as Conference Coordinator of Christian Social Involvement and Christian Global Concerns, and the Charlotte District Nominations Committee. She has taught in several Conference Schools of Christian Mission, and she served as Local Arrangements Coordinator for the South Atlantic School of Christian Mission meeting in Spartanburg, S.C.

Alec and Dot retired to Asheville, NC. Currently Dot is a member of Central United Methodist Church. Dot lost her lifelong partner of 63 years when Alec died in 2021. Dot and Alec have three adult children, Karen, Lex and Veranita, who were all born in Zimbabwe.

Dot holds a B.A. degree in Religion and Philosophy from Birmingham Southern College, her Certification for Elementary Education from Winston-Salem State University, and an M.A. degree in Early Childhood Education from Gardner Webb College.

Acknowledgment

I want to thank Jane and Margaret and many others who have helped to edit my book as the story unfolded.

I also want to thank Tanya, my daughter-in-law, and Megan, my granddaughter, for helping to publish my book, which I am profoundly grateful.

Finally, I want to thank my family who has shared my dream of publishing my book for so many years.

Printed in the USA
CPSIA information can be obtained
at www.ICGtesting.com
JSHW010453130823
46347JS00005B/136